Learning to Pass

New CLAIT

2006

Unit 1

Ruksana Patel

www.heinemann.co.uk
✓ Free online support
✓ Useful weblinks
✓ 24 hour online ordering

01865 888058

Inspiring generations

Heinemann Educational Publishers
Halley Court, Jordan Hill, Oxford OX2 8EJ
Part of Harcourt Education

Heinemann is the registered trademark of Harcourt Education Limited

Text © Ruksana Patel, 2005

First published 2005

10 09 08 07 06 05

10 9 8 7 6 5 4 3 2 1

British Library Cataloguing in Publication Data is available from the British Library on request.

10-digit ISBN: 0 435082 57 4
13-digit ISBN: 978 0 435082 57 4

Typeset by Thomson Digital, India

Original illustrations © Harcourt Education Limited, 2005

Cover design by Wooden Ark

Printed in the UK at Bath Press

Cover photo: © Getty Images

Acknowledgements
Every effort has been made to contact copyright holders of material reproduced in this book. Any omissions will be rectified in subsequent printings if notice is given to the publishers.

The author would like to express her deep gratitude and appreciation to Abdul Patel for working through the book several times and for his support, incredible patience and invaluable feedback during the writing of this book. A special thank you to Fayaz and Fozia Roked for their help, encouragement, support and for providing inspiration for the assignments. Thank you to Samiah Ismail for providing some of the digital pictures used in this book. Thank you to Elaine Tuffery, Lewis Birchon, Gavin Fidler and Susan Ross. Finally, thank you to Penny Hill for her advice and continued support.

The publisher would like to thank Daydream Education (tel. 0800 068 0232 web. www.daydreameducation.co.uk) for kind permission to reproduce the image on p17 and p38

Microsoft product screen shot(s) reprinted with permission from Microsoft Corporation.

Picture credits
All images on the CD-ROM file handout.pdf © Getty/Photodisc
Page 4 © Corbis
Page 5 © Corbis
Page 6 (top) © Corbis

Contents

Introduction to New CLAiT

This book has been designed to cover the syllabus for Unit 1 File management and e-document production of the OCR Level 1 Certificate/ Diploma for IT Users (New CLAiT) and can also be used as a basis for learning the skills for the iTQ qualification. Unit 1 is the core unit and is required by candidates who would like to achieve the Level 1 Certificate or Diploma for IT Users (New CLAiT).

Learning outcomes for Unit 1: File management and e-document production

A candidate following a programme of learning leading to this unit will be able to:

- *identify and use a computer workstation and appropriate system software*
- *use a computer's system software to create and manage files and folders*
- *identify and use word processing software correctly to enter text, numbers and symbols accurately*
- *format basic paragraph and document properties.*

New CLAiT

The OCR Level 1 Certificate/Diploma for IT Users (New CLAiT) is a qualification designed to recognise the skills, knowledge and understanding of IT users in employment, education or training. It aims to provide a nationally recognised standard in IT assessment that is accessible and flexible while also being reliable, consistent and valid. It is designed to fit the needs of the learner, employer and training provider.

The redeveloped qualification

New CLAiT has been redeveloped to produce a qualification that provides a clear progression route to Level 2 at both unit level and whole qualification level. It will equip learners with the range of transferable skills necessary to meet the demands of the modern workplace, and will prepare learners for progression to further training and accreditation in IT User Skills at Level 2.

The new qualification maps to the National Occupational Standards for IT Users created by e-skills UK. This takes account of recent software developments and provides greater flexibility, ease of use and relevance.

Aims of the qualification

The qualification aims to develop:

- *knowledge of standard IT hardware and software and the ability to operate equipment correctly and safely*
- *knowledge of a range of different software applications and the ability to use different applications effectively to complete tasks*
- *ability to manage documents and data in a variety of applications*
- *ability to enter data accurately*
- *skills and knowledge in contexts that are directly relevant to employment situations*
- *progression by assisting in the development of skills and knowledge that learners will need to undertake further study.*

Structure of the qualification

UNIT STATUS	UNIT TITLE
Core unit	Unit 1 File management and e-document production
Optional units	Unit 2 Creating spreadsheets and graphs Unit 3 Database manipulation Unit 4 e-publication creation Unit 5 Create an e-presentation Unit 6 e-image creation Unit 7 Web page creation Unit 8 Online communication Unit 9 Computing fundamentals (IC^3) Unit 10 Key applications (IC^3) Unit 11 Living online (IC^3)

All units are equally weighted. Candidates may work towards the units in any particular order and learning programmes can be tailored to meet individual needs.

Guided learning hours

An average candidate with the stated recommended prior learning suggested by OCR should take around 20 guided learning hours per unit to acquire the knowledge, understanding and skills necessary to pass that unit. However, this figure is for guidance only and will vary depending on individual candidates and the mode of learning.

Recommended prior learning

There are no minimum entry requirements, however, candidates will find it beneficial to have some entry level IT skills. New CLAiT has been designed to be accessible to learners who are entirely new to using IT and as such it is common for it to accredit the first learning journey a candidate may make in IT.

Candidate profile

New CLAiT caters for the full range of learners in IT, whether in school, college, training, further education or employment. It is ideally suited for those who have had only a very basic introduction to the use of IT, are working at Level 1, and who wish to gain accreditation for newly acquired skills at this level.

Assessment

Units 1 to 8 are assessed in a centre by a centre assessor and are then externally moderated by an OCR examiner-moderator. OCR sets the assessments. Candidates are allowed a notional duration of 2½ hours for each assessment. If candidates do not pass at the first attempt, they may have other attempts at a unit using a different OCR-set assignment. In order to achieve a unit pass, candidates must make no critical errors and no more than four accuracy errors. For detailed marking criteria, please refer to the OCR Level 1 Certificate/Diploma for IT Users New CLAiT Tutor's Handbook.

Certification

Candidates may achieve individual unit certificates, an OCR Level 1 Certificate for IT Users (New CLAiT) or an OCR Level 1 Diploma for IT Users (New CLAiT).

Each unit is regarded as a worthwhile achievement in its own right. Candidates have the option of achieving as many or as few units as are appropriate for their own learning needs or employment situation. Candidates will be awarded a unit certificate for each individual unit achieved.

To achieve the Level 1 Certificate for IT Users qualification, candidates are required to achieve **three** units, including the core unit (Unit 1).

Candidates who achieve **five** units, including the core unit (Unit 1), will be awarded an OCR Level 1 Diploma for IT Users (New CLAiT).

Progression

New CLAiT is part of a suite of qualifications in IT User skills offered by OCR. Other IT User qualifications offered by OCR are Level 2 (CLAiT Plus) and Level 3 (CLAiT Advanced).

Candidates who are successful in achieving accreditation at Level 1 will be able to progress to the OCR Level 2 Certificate/Diploma for IT Users. New CLAiT also provides a basis for progression to the NVQs which form part of the iTQ suite, NVQ Levels 1, 2 and 3 for IT Users.

Introduction to iTQ

This book covers the syllabus for Unit 1 of New CLAiT. The skills you are learning through this study are important for employment; skills in the use of IT are needed in 9 out of 10 new jobs in the UK. This foreword explains how you can make your study even more valuable. Your successful completion of this CLAiT unit can contribute to achieving an iTQ, and your progress towards an iTQ (including your completion of this CLAiT unit) can be recorded in an e-skills Passport.

The iTQ qualification and e-skills Passport

Both the iTQ and the e-skills Passport have been created by employers. The **iTQ** is a flexible IT user qualification and training package that can be tailored to ensure you are trained in the IT skills that you need for your job. The iTQ is the new National Vocational Qualification (NVQ) for IT Users. It forms part of the new Apprenticeship Framework for IT Users and is based on the e-skills UK[1] National Occupational Standards.

The **e-skills Passport** is an online tool which helps you build your IT user skills profile. The e-skills Passport provides a simple means for you to assess the level of your IT skills, plan your iTQ and demonstrate your progress and achievements to date. It is not a qualification, nor is it a formal appraisal system but it is a means to steer you towards the right mix of training and/or qualifications that suit you and your employer. This will give you your personal record of achievement, presented in a form that is widely understand and recognised by employers.

Although the e-skills Passport provides an essential understanding of the IT user skills you need prior to undertaking iTQ, it is also recommended before embarking on New CLAiT 2006. For more information visit the e-skills Passport web site (www.e-skillspassport.com).

---

[1] e-skills UK is the Sector Skills Council for IT and Telecoms (www.e-skills.com)

New CLAiT 2006 and the iTQ

New CLAiT 2006 units can contribute towards the optional units for the iTQ qualification at level 1 as shown in the table below. The knowledge, understanding and skills content for New CLAiT 2006 units are also based on the National Occupational Standards.

e-skills UK units	New CLAiT 2006 Units
Operate a computer 1(OPU1)	Unit 1 File management and e-document production
Word processing 1 (WP1)	Unit 4 e-publication creation
Spreadsheet software 1 (SS1)	Unit 2 Creating spreadsheets and graphs
Database software 1(DB1)	Unit 3 Database manipulation
Email 1 (MAIL1)	Unit 8 Online communication
Presentation software (PS1)	Unit 5 Create an e-presentation
Website software 1 (WEB1)	Unit 7 Web page creation
Artwork and imaging software 1 (ART1)	Unit 6 e-image creation

This book covers the syllabus for Unit OPU1: Operate a computer of the iTQ at Level 1. You can use other units from CLAiT Plus 2006 and New CLAiT 2006 (which are published in Heinemann's *Learning to Pass New CLAiT/CLAiT Plus* 2006 series) as well as other popular IT user qualifications to count towards your iTQ.

Therefore, if you are embarking on the iTQ and you have selected this unit then this book can provide the underpinning knowledge required to help you to successfully complete the unit.

The iTQ Calculator

The iTQ can be achieved at three levels. Each component unit at each level has been allocated a number of points. The tables below also show the total number of points that need to be achieved for iTQ at each level. You can select units from different levels in order to achieve the desired number of points, provided you take the mandatory unit (Make selective use of IT) and at least 60% of your unit choices are at the iTQ level that you wish to achieve.

	iTQ LEVELS		
	Level 1	Level 2	Level 3
Total required	40	100	180
Total of points to come from optional units at level of qualification	15	40	75

For example, for a Level 1 qualification:

- *Overall points total of 40*
- *15 points come from mandatory unit*
- *25 points come from optional units*
- *Of the 25 optional points 15 must be achieved at Level 1*

iTQ internal credit matrix

Unit Titles	Unit Values		
	Level 1	Level 2	Level 3
Mandatory unit			
Make selective use of IT	15	25	35
Optional units			
Using IT systems	5	15	25
Operate a computer	10	20	30
IT trouble shooting for users	5	15	25
IT maintenance for users	5	15	25
IT security for users	5	15	25
Use IT to exchange information	5	15	25
Internets and intranets	5	15	25
Email	5	15	25
Word processing	10	20	30
Spreadsheets	10	20	35
Databases	10	20	35
Websites	10	20	35
IT artwork and images	10	20	35
IT presentations	10	20	30
Specialist or bespoke software	10	20	30
Evaluate the impact of IT	5	15	25
Sector specific unit	10	20	30

For more information about iTQ, visit the iTQ web site (www.itq.org.uk)

Who this book is suitable for

This book is suitable for:

- *candidates working towards: OCR Level 1 Certificate or Diploma for IT Users (New CLAiT), and OCR iTQ qualification*

- *complete beginners, with no prior knowledge of Windows XP or Word 2003*

- *use as a self-study workbook – the user should work through the book from start to finish*

- *tutor-assisted workshops or tutor-led groups*

- *individuals wanting to learn to use Windows XP and Microsoft Word 2003*

Although this book is based on Windows XP and Word 2003, it is also suitable for users of Word 2002 (XP) and Word 2000. Note that a few of the skills may be slightly different and some screenshots will not be identical.

Chapter 1 — Learning to use a computer and file management

For the first part of Unit 1, you will need to understand how to use a computer safely and how to manage files and folders.

To learn the basics of using a computer, we will use Windows XP. There are two different versions of Windows XP: Windows XP Professional and Windows XP Home Edition. You can use this book for either version of Windows XP.

This chapter is divided into two sections:

○ *in Section 1, you will learn about the different parts of a computer and basic health and safety practices when using a computer*

○ *in Section 2, you will learn how to manage computer files and folders.*

How to work through this chapter

1 Read the explanation of a term first.

2 If there are some terms you do not understand, refer to Unit 1 Definition of terms on page 114.

3 Work through the chapter in sequence so that one skill is understood before moving on to the next. This ensures understanding of the topic and prevents mistakes.

4 Read the ▶ *How to...* guidelines which give step-by-step instructions for each skill. Do not attempt to work through the How to... guidelines, read through each point and look at the screenshots. Make sure you understand all the instructions before moving on.

5 To make sure that you have understood how to perform a skill, work through the Check your understanding task following that skill. You should refer to the How to... guidelines when doing the task.

6 At the end of each section, there is an Assess your skills table. This lists the skills that you will have practised by working through each section. Look at each item listed to help you decide whether you are confident that you can perform each skill.

7 Towards the end of the book are Quick reference guides, Build-up and Practice tasks. Work through each of the tasks.

If you need help, you may refer to the How to... guidelines or Quick reference guides whilst doing the Build-up tasks. Whilst working on the Practice task, you should feel confident enough to use only the Quick reference guides if you need support. These guides may also be used during an assessment.

A CD-ROM accompanies this book. On it are the files that you will need to use for the file management tasks. Instructions for copying the files are provided at the beginning of Chapter 1 Section 2 on page 25. The solutions for all the tasks can be found in a folder called **worked_copies_unit1**

Note: there are many ways of performing the skills covered in this book. This book provides How to... guidelines that are easily understood by learners.

1: Use a computer

LEARNING OUTCOMES

In this section you will learn how to:

- understand and use computer hardware and software
- understand health and safety practices when using a computer
- switch on a computer and monitor
- understand windows, icons, buttons, menus and toolbars
- use a password
- use a mouse
- use a keyboard
- shut down the computer.

What is a computer?

A computer is a machine that is capable of taking in and processing information (referred to as data) at speed without making errors. A machine works the way it is programmed to function – it does not make mistakes. A computer is often referred to as a PC, which stands for personal computer. Remember, it is almost impossible to break a computer by using it and it is quite easy to correct any mistakes that you make. So don't be afraid to use a computer!

You will need to understand:

- *how a computer works*
- *the difference between hardware and software*
- *the different ways of storing data.*

The following pages give a brief introduction. These topics are covered in more detail on a separate handout called 'Unit 1 Handout Understanding Computers', which can be found on the CD-ROM accompanying this book.

Nowadays, many people use a laptop because it has the advantage of being portable.

FIGURE 1.1 A laptop computer is convenient and portable

FIGURE 1.2 A typical computer system

What does it mean?

Hardware
Hardware are the physical parts that you can see and touch.
Software
Software are computer programs that allow you to use the computer, such as Microsoft Word. You cannot touch software.

Monitor
Also referred to as **VDU (Visual Display Unit)** or screen because it looks like a television screen. Allows you to see data being entered into the computer.
The angle/position may be adjusted to suit you. May have an on/off switch and other settings buttons to allow you to change brightness etc. Thin, flat screen monitors are also available

Keyboard
Used to enter (input) information into the computer. Has more than 100 keys, including letters arranged in a set pattern, numbers and symbols.

Central Processing Unit (CPU) box
The most important part of a computer.
Contains the **memory** (brain).
Contains the hard disk drive which stores programs and data.
Other parts: printer, monitor, keyboard, mouse are connected using cables to the CPU box.
The CPU can be horizontal or upright as shown. An upright box is referred to as a tower.

Mouse
Should be placed on a mousemat.
As you move the mouse on the mousemat, a pointer moves in the same direction on the screen.
Allows you to point at things on the screen and click.
A typical mouse has two buttons, a left and a right button.

Printer
Allows what is seen on screen to be printed on paper, referred to as hard copy. Many types of printer are available, e.g. laser, inkjet.
Some print in black and white only.
Printers need ink cartridges and paper to print.

CD-ROM drive

On/off switch

Floppy disk drive

Zip disk drive (not on all computers)

Speakers

Storing data

Data that is input into a computer can be saved to a variety of storage devices, as shown in the table below.

STORAGE DEVICE		DESCRIPTION
Hard disk		A fixed storage medium. A hard disk drive is usually inbuilt into the CPU box. Hard disk drives can store large amounts of data. On a networked computer system there are often many different drives, each one is given a letter.
Compact disc (CD)		A removable, portable, storage medium that holds large amounts of data but not as much as a hard disk. Types of CD are: ● CD-R – data can be saved on to it but cannot be deleted ● CD-RW – data can be saved, updated and deleted ● CD-ROM – data can be read only, e.g. software programs.
Floppy disk		A floppy disk drive can be inbuilt into the CPU box or it can be an external drive. A floppy disk drive is often called the (A:) drive. A 3½ inch disk is inserted into the floppy disk drive and data can be saved on to it. The advantage of this removable storage medium is that it is portable and easy to use – it can be inserted and used in any computer that has a floppy disk drive. However, it can only store a limited amount of data.
USB disk		Also referred to as Flash Disk/Memory Stick/Flash Pen. Increasingly popular, this removable storage medium can store larger amounts of data than floppy disks and is portable. It is inserted into a USB port located at the front or back of a computer.
Zip disk		Zip disks are as portable and versatile as floppy disks but have the advantage of being able to store much larger amounts of data. Zip disks need to be inserted into a zip disk drive. Not all computers have an inbuilt zip disk drive, they can be external drives.

Referring to the diagram of a typical computer system on page 5, find the different hardware parts of your computer.

1 Is the CPU box upright or horizontal? (Not applicable to laptops.)

2 Does your computer have a floppy disk drive? If so, find the floppy disk drive – it may be in a slightly different place on your computer from that shown in the diagram.

3 Find the eject button which is usually under the floppy disk drive.

4 Does your computer have a CD-ROM drive? Not all computers do. Similarly, your computer may not have a zip disk drive. Find the button that allows you to open and close the CD-ROM drive.

5 Find the on/off switch on the CPU box (don't switch it on just yet!).

6 Does your monitor have an on/off switch? Are the buttons to adjust settings, e.g. brightness/contrast, at the front of your monitor? Are you able to adjust the positioning of the monitor? Be careful whenever you adjust the monitor, as the wires at the back may not be fully secure.

7 Find the mouse. Position your wrist over the mouse, keep the mouse on the mousemat and move it around slowly on the mat to get the feel of it. If your mouse has a cord, do not pull too hard as the wire may not be fully secure.

8 Does your computer have external speakers? They may be inbuilt into the computer.

9 Find the keyboard. Tap on the keys to get a feel for using the keyboard.

10 Find the printer. It may not be next to the computer. Is it a printer that will be used by more than one computer? If so, this is a shared printer.

Health and safety

When you use a computer, you should be aware of safe working practices to reduce the risk of strain-type injuries.

▶▶ How to... protect your eyes

○ *Use a monitor that:*
  • *is adjustable*
  • *has an inbuilt or additional anti-glare screen to protect your eyes*
  • *is positioned below your line of sight – you should be looking down at the monitor.*
○ *You should look away from the screen approximately every ten minutes to avoid eye strain.*

▶▶ How to... be aware of your posture

- Use a chair that can swivel and has an adjustable height.
- Your back and elbows should be supported.
- Both of your feet should touch the floor.
- Your knees and elbows should be at a 90-degree angle.

▶▶ How to... avoid repetitive strain injury (RSI)

- RSI can be caused if the keyboard or mouse are used incorrectly over a long period of time.
- RSI may affect the fingers, wrists, elbows and lower arms.
- When using a computer, make sure that your wrists are relaxed. Your wrists must be higher than your fingers, not lower.
- It may be helpful to use a wrist support in front of your keyboard and/or on your mousemat.

FIGURE 1.3 Check that you are seated correctly at the computer

Check your understanding *Basic health and safety*

1 Sit at your computer workstation.

2 Make sure your chair is at the correct height and angle. Your back should be straight and your feet should be flat on the floor.

3 Make sure that there is no glare on the screen.

4 Adjust the angle of the monitor. Your head should not be tilted back to look up at the screen.

Starting the computer

▶▶ How to... *switch on the computer*

Before you switch on a computer, you will need to check a few things.

- *Make sure that the light on the CPU box (or laptop) is not already on.*
  - *Some computers go on standby, so the light will be on even though nothing displays on screen. In that case, move the mouse or press any key on the keyboard. You should not press the on/off switch.*
- *Make sure that there is no disk in the floppy disk drive. If there is, press the eject button to remove it.*
- *When a computer is switched on, it will boot up (load up). The computer prepares itself for use by carrying out various checks, for example, the central processing unit checks that the monitor, keyboard, mouse and printer are all connected correctly.*
- *The monitor may switch on automatically when the computer is switched on. If not, you will need to press the on/off switch on the monitor.*

Check your understanding *Start the computer*

1 Start up your computer and monitor.

2 A login screen or desktop is displayed.

3 If a login screen is displayed (Figure 1.4), prompting you to enter your user password (or user name and password), work through 'The start-up screen' and 'Passwords' sections on pages 10–11.

FIGURE 1.4 An example of a login screen

FIGURE 1.5 An example of a computer desktop

4 If the desktop screen is displayed (Figure 1.5), work through 'The windows desktop' section on pages 11–12.

The start-up screen

- *When you start up your computer, a screen telling you to press* **Ctrl + Alt + Delete** *may display.*
- *Find these three keys on your keyboard.*
- *Press all three keys at the same time.*
- *Another screen prompting you to enter your user name and/or password may be displayed.*

Passwords

If your computer is networked:

- *you are usually told the user name that you will need to use*
- *you may be given a password or asked to choose your own.*

If your computer is stand-alone:

- *it may be set up so that you do not have to enter a user name and/or password every time you log in*
- *you may have a choice for your user name and password.*

▶▶ How to... *choose a password*

- A good password should consist of a combination of letters and numbers so that others cannot guess it.
- Avoid using obvious passwords such as your birthday or your car registration.
- On some computer systems your password may need to be a minimum number of characters.
- Passwords may be case sensitive (you may need to use lower case and/ or upper case letters).
- Passwords should be changed from time to time for security reasons.
- Passwords should not be given to other users for security reasons.
- Passwords may be used on a drive, a folder or a file to protect confidential information.

▶▶ How to... *use a password to log in to a computer*

1 On the login screen, click on the **User Name** box.

2 Use the keyboard to enter your user name.

3 Click in the **Password** box.

4 Enter your password using the keyboard. Make sure you use lower and/or upper case correctly.

5 The password appears on-screen as dots so that others cannot see it.

6 Click on **OK** or the green arrow to proceed.

7 The computer will load up (boot up) and the computer desktop will be displayed.

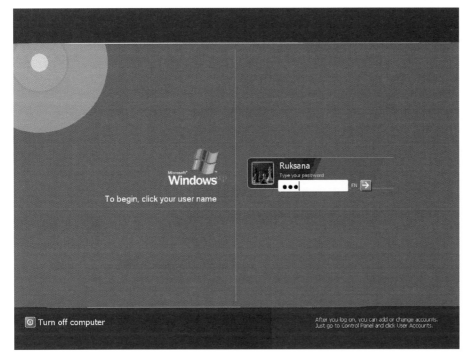

FIGURE 1.6 Your user name and password screen may be different to this one

Check your understanding
Enter your user name and/or password

1 Enter your user name and/or password (as required by the computer).

2 Make sure no one can see the keyboard when you enter the password.

The Windows desktop

Windows uses a **Graphical User Interface (GUI)**. This shows **icons** (small pictures) and **menus** (lists of items). Windows operating systems are easy to use, when you click with your mouse on an icon or menu item, you are actually giving the computer a command (or instruction) to do something.

When you start up your computer, the **desktop** screen is displayed (Figure 1.7). This is the work area for all tasks performed in Windows.

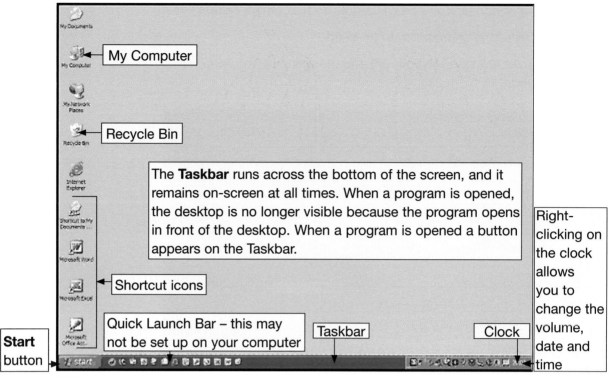

FIGURE 1.7 A desktop screen

Do not worry if your desktop screen is not identical to the screen prints shown in this book. The desktop icons, desktop background and the programs on the **Start** menu will vary from one computer to another, but the basic layout is very similar.

The desktop background may be a plain colour (as in Figure 1.7) or may have a picture as the background. Backgrounds can be changed in the **Control Panel**.

A program can be opened in various ways:

- *through the **Start** menu*
- *by double-clicking the shortcut icons on the desktop*
- *by single-clicking on the program icon on the **Quick Launch bar** if a shortcut has been created.*

The mouse

 *use a mouse*

The mouse lets the computer know what you want it to do. A standard mouse works better if placed on a mousemat. This provides a smooth, non-slip surface. The mouse ball gathers dust and should be cleaned periodically.

Make sure the mouse cord is pointing away from you, then rest your hand on the mouse as shown in Figure 1.8. Left-handed users may place the

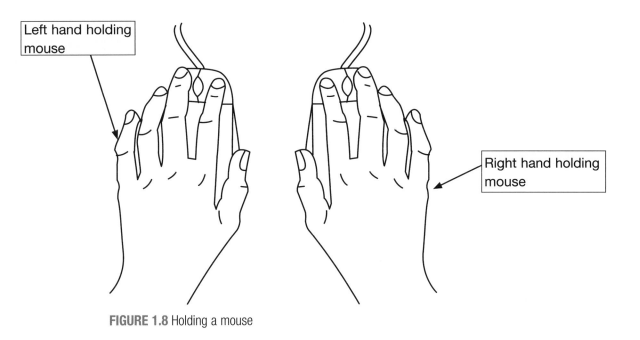

Left hand holding mouse

Right hand holding mouse

FIGURE 1.8 Holding a mouse

mouse to the left of the keyboard and can also change the button settings in the **Control Panel**.

Think of the mouse as an extension of your hand – you don't look at your hand when you use it, instead you feel what you are doing. When you use the mouse, you should look at the computer screen not at your hand.

MOUSE ACTION	DESCRIPTION
Point	Move the mouse on the mousemat until the pointer appears at the required position on the screen
Click	Press and release the **left** mouse button once
Double-Click	Quickly press the left mouse button **twice,** then release it.
Right-Click	Press the **right** mouse button once, a menu displays
Hover	Position the mouse pointer over an icon or menu item and pause, a toolbar **Tool tip** or a further menu item will appear (Figure 1.9). Save (Ctrl+S) FIGURE 1.9 Save **Tool tip** in Microsoft Word

Mouse techniques

Note: unless otherwise instructed, always click using the left mouse button.

Make sure that the computer is switched on and the desktop screen is displayed.

Hold the mouse

1 Place your hand over the mouse.

2 Use your thumb to hold the left side of the mouse and your little finger to hold the right side (left-handers reverse this instruction).

3 Position your forefinger on the left mouse button, but don't click the button!

Move the mouse

1 Still holding the mouse, look at the screen and move the mouse to the left slowly. Notice that the pointer on the screen moves to the left.

2 Move the mouse to the right slowly. Notice that the pointer moves to the right.

3 The mouse pointer on the screen moves in response to the direction that you move the mouse on the mousemat.

Select and deselect

1 Move the mouse pointer over the **My Computer** icon on the desktop screen. Click once on this icon, it becomes highlighted (different shade) – the icon has been selected.

2 Move the mouse pointer away from the **My Computer** icon to a blank part of the screen.

3 Click once – this deselects the **My Computer** icon, it is no longer highlighted.

Right-click

1 Move the mouse to a blank area on the desktop screen.

2 Right-click with the mouse.

FIGURE 1.10 Right-click on the mouse to see a menu

3 A menu (list of items) is displayed when you right-click (Figure 1.10).

4 Click in a blank part of the desktop screen.

5 The menu disappears.

Mouse pointers

Windows uses different types of mouse pointer. The type of pointer displayed indicates what the computer is doing at the time.

POINTER	NAME	WHAT IT DOES
	Arrow	Used to point and click at things
	I-beam	Appears in a Word document, so you can click to place it between letters. Also referred to as a cursor
	Busy	Usually looks like an hourglass. This shows that the computer is taking time to do something, wait until the busy sign finishes
	Resize	Drag to resize a window, changes depending on where it is placed. Can be diagonal, vertical or horizontal
	Move	Used to move pictures or objects around a page

Types of mouse pointer

The Start button

The **Start** button is located at the bottom left of the desktop screen. This button can be used to start any program that is installed on the computer.

Make sure the computer is switched on and the desktop screen is displayed.

1 Hover the mouse over the **Start** button.

2 A **Tool tip, Click here to begin** Click here to begin , is displayed.

3 Click on **Start**.

4 The **Windows XP Start** menu appears.

5 Look at the programs on the **Start** menu. The contents of the **Start** menus shown in Figure 1.11 and Figure 1.12 may be different on your computer. The list on the left of the Start menu shows recently used programs. These will also vary between computers.

FIGURE 1.11 A Start menu

FIGURE 1.12 A different Start menu

6 Click anywhere on the desktop screen away from the **Start** menu to remove the **Start** menu from the screen (or click on the **Start** button again).

The keyboard

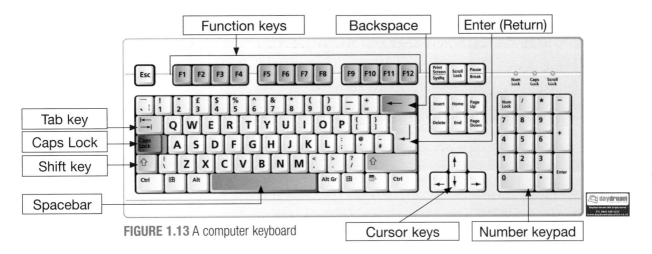

FIGURE 1.13 A computer keyboard

Some of the symbols and keys may be in a different place on the keyboard you are using.

▶▶ **How to...** *use the keyboard*

HOW TO...	ACTION
See where text will be entered	Look for the flashing straight line on the screen. Your text will be entered wherever this line is. This is the cursor (or I-beam)
Type one capital letter	Hold down the Shift key and press the required letter on the keyboard, then let go of the Shift key
Type word(s) in capital letters	Press down the Caps Lock to switch it on (a light may indicate that Caps Lock is on)
Type lower case letters	Check the Caps Lock is switched off. If not press down the Caps Lock key to turn it off
Insert a space between words	Press the Spacebar on the keyboard once
Delete a letter to the left of the cursor	Press the Backspace key
Delete a letter to the right of the cursor	Press the Delete key
Move to the next line	Press the Enter key
Move to the beginning of the line	Press the Home key
Move to the end of the line	Press the End key
Move to the beginning of the document	Press the Ctrl and Home keys at the same time
Move to the end of the document	Press the Ctrl and End keys at the same time
Create a new paragraph	Press Enter twice at the end of a paragraph. This will display one clear line space between two paragraphs

Using the keyboard

Symbols on the keyboard

● *To enter a symbol which appears on the top half of a key on the keyboard, hold the* **Shift** *key down, press the key on the keyboard while still holding the* **Shift** *key, then let go of the* **Shift** *key.*

● *To enter a symbol which appears on the lower half of a key, tap that key.*

SYMBOL	DESCRIPTION
.	Full stop
,	Comma
:	Colon
;	Semi-colon
(	Opening bracket
)	Closing bracket
=	Equals sign
_	Underscore – hold down the **Shift** key to enter an underscore (underscore is different from hyphen/dash)
?	Question mark
"	Speech marks
' ' '	Single quote mark and apostrophe
-	Hyphen or dash
+	Plus sign
*	Star (asterisk)
/	Forward slash
\	Back slash
@	At symbol
&	Ampersand (and)
!	Exclamation mark
£	Pound sign
#	Hash
%	Percentage sign
<	Less than symbol
>	Greater than symbol

Keyboard symbols

To practise using the keyboard, you will use Microsoft Word 2003.

▶▶ How to... *Start Microsoft Word 2003*

Make sure that the computer is switched on and the desktop screen is displayed.

1   Click on **Start**.

2   The **Windows XP Start** menu is displayed (Figure 1.14).

3   Click on **All Programs**.

4   The **All Programs** menu appears.

5   Click on **Microsoft Office**.

6   A list of Microsoft Office programs is displayed.

7   Click on **Microsoft Office Word 2003**.

8   A blank Microsoft Word document is displayed (Figure 1.15).

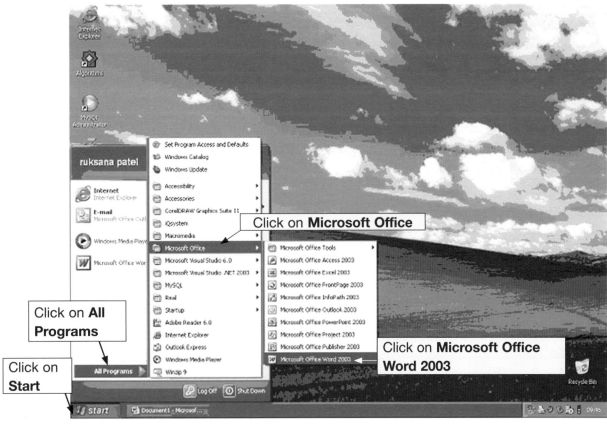

FIGURE 1.14 Starting Microsoft Word 2003

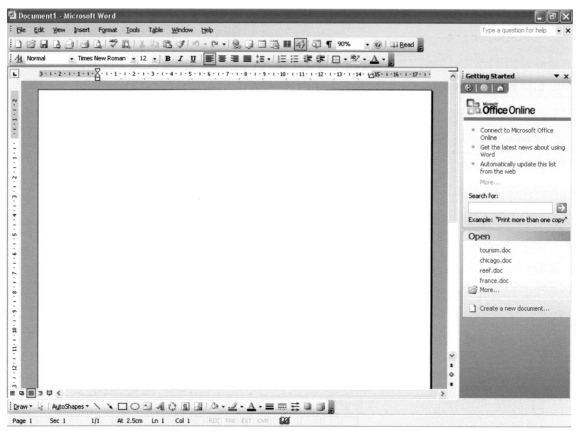

FIGURE 1.15 A blank Microsoft Word document

The Microsoft Word window will be covered in more detail in Chapter 2 (see page 47). For now you are simply going to use this document to practise your keyboard skills.

Check your understanding *Use the keyboard*

Refer to 'How to... Use the Keyboard' on page 17.

1 A blank Microsoft Word document should be open on your screen.

2 In the document, look for the flashing vertical line in the top left of the screen. This is the **cursor**. It indicates the position where text will be entered.

Enter text

Ignore any errors that you may make for the moment!

1 Practise using the keyboard by pressing some of the alphabet keys.

2 Press the **Enter** key to start a new line.

3 Press the **Shift** key, keep it held down and enter the first letter of your first name.

4 Let go of the **Shift** key and enter the rest of your first name.

5 Press the **Spacebar.**

6 Hold the **Shift** key, keep it held down and enter the first letter of your last name.

7 Let go of the **Shift** key and enter the rest of your last name.

8 Press the **Enter** key.

9 Press the **Caps Lock** key to switch it on, and enter the name of the town/city that you live in.

10 Press the **Enter** key twice.

Enter numbers

1 Enter some numbers by pressing the number keys above the alphabet keys.

2 Press the **Num Lock** key to switch the number keypad on.

3 Enter some numbers using the number keypad.

4 Press the **Enter** key twice.

Enter symbols

Refer to the **Keyboard symbols** chart on page 17.

1 Hold down the **Shift** key and enter the symbols displayed above the alphabet keys. Let go of the Shift key.

2 Enter the symbols that appear on other parts of the keyboard, e.g. / (forward slash), = (equals sign).

3 Use the **Shift** key and enter the symbols displayed on the top half of a key, e.g. £ (pound sign), + (plus sign).

4 Practise typing the commonly used symbols: , (comma) . (full stop) : (colon) ; (semi-colon) ? (question mark).

Delete text

1 Click with your mouse in the top row of text in your document.

2 Press the **Delete** key. This deletes text to the **right** of the cursor.

3 Click with your mouse at the end of the last line in your document.

4 Press the **Backspace** key. This deletes text to the **left** of the cursor.

Now, try moving around the page. Refer to 'How to... Use the keyboard' on page 17 to help you do this.

Close and exit a Word document without saving

As the Word document you have been working on is only a practice document, you do not need to save it.

▶▶ How to... close a document without saving

1 In your Word document, move the mouse to the red cross ☒ in the top right corner of the screen.

2 Click on ☒.

3 A **Microsoft Office Word** dialogue box is displayed.

4 Click on **No** (Figure 1.16).

5 The Word document closes and the desktop screen is displayed.

What does it mean?

Dialogue box
A dialogue box is a window that displays options, such as OK and Cancel.

Shutting down the computer

When you have finished using the computer you should:

- *close any files that are open*
- *then close all programs*
- *and, finally, shut down the operating system (or log off).*

The shut down process may vary slightly on different computer systems, but the basic process is similar. You will need to either shut down the computer or turn off the computer.

Microsoft Office Word

⚠ Do you want to save the changes to Document1?

[Yes]   [No]   [Cancel]

FIGURE 1.16 Click on **No**.

▶▶ How to... shut down the computer

1 In the desktop screen, click on **Start**.

2 The **Windows XP Start** menu is displayed.

3 Click on **Shut Down** (Figure 1.17).

FIGURE 1.17 The **Shut Down** button in the **Start** menu

4 The **Shut Down Windows** dialogue box is displayed (Figure 1.18).

5 In the **What do you want the computer to do?** box, click on the drop-down arrow and select **Shut down**.

6 Click on **OK**.

7 The computer will switch off.

8 Switch off the monitor if required.

▶▶ How to... *turn off the computer*

1 In the desktop screen, click on **Start**.

2 The **Start** menu is displayed.

3 Click on **Turn Off Computer** (Figure 1.19).

4 The **Turn off computer** dialogue box is displayed (Figure 1.20).

5 Click on **Turn Off**.

6 The computer will shut down.

7 Switch off the monitor if required.

FIGURE 1.18 Shut Down Windows dialogue box

FIGURE 1.19 Turn Off Computer button

TIP!

Never press the on/off button on the computer or the plug at the electric wall socket if the desktop screen is displayed. Always close all open windows and shut down or log off your computer correctly.

FIGURE 1.20 Turn off computer dialogue box

Check your understanding *Shut down the computer*

1 Close any open windows.

2 Shut down (or turn off) your computer.

On your computer you may be required to log off instead of shut down (or turn off).

ASSESS YOUR SKILLS – Use a computer

By working through Section 1 you will have learnt the skills below. Read each item to help you decide how confident you feel about each skill.

identify computer hardware:
- CPU box
- Monitor
- Keyboard
- Mouse
- Printer

- understand basic health and safety practices when using a computer

- start up a computer

- switch on a monitor (if required)

- use a password

- understand the desktop

- identify the **Start** button

- identify the **Taskbar**

- use a mouse

- use the keyboard

- shut down (or turn off) the computer.

If you feel you need more practice on any of the skills above, go back and work through the skill(s) again.

If you feel confident, move on to Section 2.

Files for this chapter

To work through the tasks in Section 2, you will need the files from the folder called **files_chapter1,** which you will find on the CD-ROM provided with this book. Copy this folder into your user area before you begin.

▶▶ **How to...** *copy the folder files_chapter1 from the CD-ROM*

Make sure the computer is switched on and the desktop screen is displayed.

1   Insert the CD-ROM into the CD-ROM drive of the computer.

2   Close any windows that may be open.

3   In the desktop, double-click on the **My Computer** icon.

4   The **My Computer** window is displayed.

5   Under **Devices with Removable Storage**, double-click on the **CD Drive** icon to view the contents of the CD-ROM.

6   A window displaying the contents of the CD appears.

7   Double-click on the **L1_Unit1_FM+DP** folder. Double-click on the **Source files** folder.

8   The **Source files** window is displayed (Figure 1.21).

9   Click on the folder **files_chapter1**.

10   The folder will be highlighted (usually blue).

11   In the **File and Folder Tasks** box, click on **Copy this folder**.

12   A **Copy Items** dialogue box is displayed (Figure 1.22).

13   Click on the user area where you want to copy the folder **files_chapter1**.

14   Click on **Copy**.

15   The folder **files_chapter1** will be copied to your user area.

16   It is advisable to copy and paste a second copy to another folder in your user area as backup.

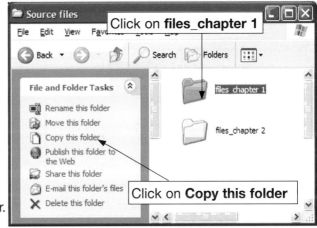

FIGURE 1.21 The Source files window

FIGURE 1.22 Copy Items dialogue box

Read only files

The files provided are set to 'read only'. After you have copied the files to your user area, remove the 'read only' properties as follows:

1 In your user area, right-click on the folder **files_chapter1**.

2 A menu appears.

3 Click on **Properties**.

4 A **Properties** dialogue box is displayed.

5 Click in the **Read-only** box to remove the tick/square (the box should be empty).

6 Click on **Apply**.

7 A **Confirm Attribute Changes** dialogue box is displayed (Figure 1.23).

8 Select **Apply changes to this folder, subfolders and files** by clicking in the second button.

9 Click on **OK**.

10 The **Confirm Attribute Changes** dialogue box closes.

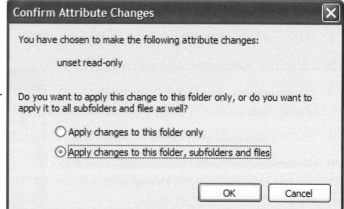

FIGURE 1.23 Confirm Attribute Changes dialogue box

11 Click on **OK** to close the **Properties** dialogue box.

2: File management

LEARNING OUTCOMES

In this section you will learn how to:

- create and name folders
- create and name subfolders
- rename files
- rename folders
- delete files
- delete folders
- move files
- copy files
- produce screen prints to show folder contents
- save screen prints.

▶▶ **How to...** *recognise folder and file icons*

ICON	WHAT IT LOOKS LIKE
Folder	
Word file	
Text file	
Image file (image file icons may vary on your computer)	

Folder and file icons

Password-protected documents

You should always be aware of the need for security when using computers. Using passwords to log in to a computer is one method of protection, another is to password-protect confidential documents.

On some computer systems you may not be prompted to enter a password when you log in; therefore you must be familiar with using passwords at other times, e.g. on a password-protected file, or folder, or a drive on the computer.

▶▶ **How to...** *use a password on a password-protected drive/folder/file (optional)*

Make sure your computer is switched on.

1 Go to the password-protected drive, file or folder.

2 Double-click on the drive, file or folder to open it.

3 You will be prompted to enter a password in the **Password** dialogue box (Figure 1.24).

4 Make sure no one can see your keyboard when you enter the password.

5 Enter the password. Use upper or lower case correctly.

6 The password appears in the box as dots for security.

7 Click on **OK**.

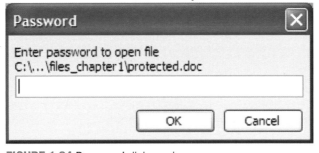

FIGURE 1.24 Password dialogue box

User area
A user area is the workspace on a computer where you save your files.

One example of a user area is a folder called **My Documents**, Windows XP creates this area. In a centre, you may be given a work area on a network. This area may have a drive name, e.g. G drive. Alternatively, you may save your work on a floppy disk, which is usually the A drive. On your own personal computer, your user area may be the C drive.

What does it mean?

File
A file is a collection of saved data. To create a word-processed file, a blank document is opened, data is entered into this document, the document is saved with a particular name, and is then referred to as a file. Files may be picture files, spreadsheet files, text files, etc.

What does it mean?

Folder
A folder is a storage area within a user area in which files can be saved. A folder may contain files and other folders (called subfolders). Creating folders with suitable names allows computer files to be stored logically. This is like organising a filing cabinet by having separate drawers, with related files in each draw. Within each drawer, files can be organised further.

1 Make sure your computer is switched on and go to your user area.

2 Double-click on the folder **files_chapter1**.

3 The contents of the **files_chapter1** folder are displayed.

4 Look for a Microsoft Word document called **protected**.

5 To open the file, double-click on it.

6 You will be prompted to enter a password.

7 Enter the password **UseAPc1**. You must use upper or lower case correctly because passwords are case sensitive.

8 Click on **OK** to open the file.

9 To close the file, click on the **red cross** ☒ in the top right corner of the Word window.

My Computer window

Windows gets its name from the fact that everything you do on a computer is shown in a window. All windows are similar.

○ *There is the **Title bar** across the top (Figure 1.25).*

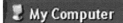

FIGURE 1.25 Title bar

○ *There are three Window control buttons in the top right corner:*
  * *Minimise* ⬛
  * *Maximise* ⬛
  * *Close* ☒
○ *If a window fills the screen, the centre button is **Restore Down** ⬛.*
  *Click on **Restore Down** to make the window smaller.*

All the tasks about working with files and folders should be done through the **My Computer** window.

1 Make sure that the computer is switched on and the desktop screen is displayed.

2 In the Windows desktop, double-click on **My Computer** .

3 The **My Computer** window is displayed.

4 Look at the examples of **My Computer** windows in Figure 1.26 and Figure 1.27 and compare them with the window on your screen – your screen may have fewer/more icons.

Menu bar	Toolbar

Title bar	Window control buttons

FIGURE 1.26 My Computer window

FIGURE 1.27 My Computer window

5 In the **My Computer** window, identify your user area.

6 Double-click on the relevant icon (or on My Documents) to go to your user area.

7 Your user area is displayed.

8 Find the folder **files_chapter1** which you copied to your user area in an earlier task.

9 Double-click on the **files_chapter1** icon to view the contents of this folder.

10 The **files_chapter1** window is displayed (Figure 1.28).

FIGURE 1.28 The files_chapter1 window

11 Remain in the **files_chapter1** window.

Viewing folder contents

- To view the contents of a folder, double-click on the folder icon. This displays any subfolders and/or files contained within the folder.

- Double-clicking on a file icon opens the file in the software that the file was created in. If you accidentally open a file, click on ▣ at the top right of the window to close it.

Check your understanding
View folder contents for files_chapter1

1 In the **files_chapter1** window, double-click on the folder icon called **try**.

2 The **try** folder is displayed.

3 Inside the **try** folder is one image file icon called **monitor**.

4 Click on **Back** | ◉ Back .

5 You will be returned to the **files_chapter1** window.

6 Double-click on the folder icon called **task1**.

7 A subfolder called **t1files** and three text file icons called **autumn, spring, summer** are displayed.

8 Double-click on the **t1files** folder icon.

9 The subfolder **t1files** is displayed. The subfolder contains an image file called **daffy** and a text file called **winter**.

10 Click on **Back**.

11 You will be returned to the **task1** folder.

12 Click on **Back** again.

13 This takes you back to the **files_chapter1** folder.

14 Click on ▣ in the top corner of the **My Computer** window to close the window.

Creating and naming folders

▶▶ How to... create and name a folder

1 On the desktop, double-click on the **My Computer** icon.

2 The **My Computer** window is displayed.

3 Double-click on the icon for your user area (or click on **My Documents** to find your user area).

4 Your user area is displayed.

5 In the **File and Folder Tasks** box, click on **Make a new folder** (Figure 1.29).

6 A **New Folder** icon is displayed (Figure 1.30). The words **New Folder** are highlighted.

7 Press the **Backspace** key to delete the highlighted words **New Folder**.

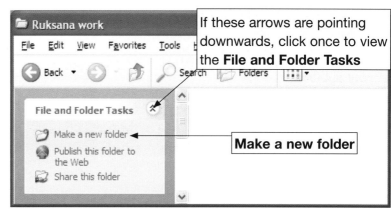

FIGURE 1.29 File and Folder Tasks box

8 Enter the required folder name (Figure 1.31).

9 Press the **Enter** key.

10 Your new folder is created.

TIP!

If the words **New Folder** are no longer highlighted or there is no flashing cursor, you may have accidentally pressed a key on the keyboard. If so, follow the instructions for 'How to... Rename a Folder' on page 34.

FIGURE 1.30 Creating a New Folder

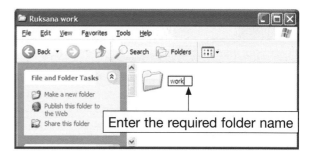

FIGURE 1.31 Naming a folder

Check your understanding *Create and name a folder*

1 Open your user area and create a new folder.

2 Name this folder **work**.

3 Remain in your user area.

Creating and naming subfolders

▶▶ *How to...* *create a subfolder*

1 In the **My Computer** window, in your user area, double-click on the folder icon in which you want to create a subfolder.

2 The folder contents are displayed (the folder may be empty).

3 In the **File and Folder Tasks** box, click on **Make a new folder**.

4 A **New Folder** icon is displayed. This will be your subfolder.

5 Press the **Backspace** key to delete the highlighted words **New Folder**.

6 Enter the required subfolder name.

7 Press the **Enter** key.

8 Your new subfolder is created (Figure 1.32).

FIGURE 1.32 Creating a subfolder

Check your understanding *Create and name a subfolder*

1 In your user area, create a subfolder in the folder **work**.

2 Name this subfolder **chapter1**.

3 Click on ☒ to close the folder **work** and return to your user area.

File extensions

Before you begin the section on renaming a file, you will need to check whether file extensions are displayed on your computer.

◉ *In your user area, open the folder **files_chapter1**.*

◉ *Are file extensions displayed after the filename? In Figure 1.33 a filename is shown with an extension, whereas in Figure 1.34 the filename has no extension.*

FIGURE 1.33 Filename with extension

FIGURE 1.34 Filename with no extension

What does it mean?

File extension
This is a dot and three or four characters after a filename, which shows the file type. The characters will be different depending on the file type. For example, the file extension of:
◉ a Word file is **.doc**
◉ a text file is **.txt**
◉ an image (picture) file can be **.gif** or **.jpg**
◉ an Excel spreadsheet is **.xls**.

If file extensions are displayed on your computer, you will need to remove them before starting 'How to... rename a file'.

▶▶ How to... *remove the display of file extensions*

1 In the folder **files_chapter1**, click on the **Tools** menu.

2 From the menu, select **Folder Options**.

3 The **Folder Options** dialogue box is displayed.

4 To open the **View** option, click on the **View** tab (Figure 1.35).

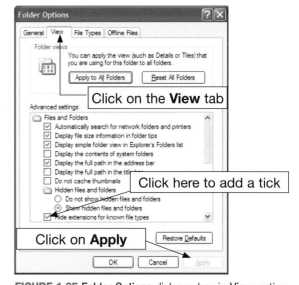

FIGURE 1.35 Folder Options dialogue box in View option

5 Click in the **Hide extensions for known file types** box to add a tick.

6 Click on **Apply**.

7 Click on **OK**.

Renaming files

▶▶ How to... *rename a file*

1 In the **My Computer** window, in your user area, double-click on the folder containing the file to be renamed.

2 The folder opens.

3 Click on the file to be renamed.

4 The file is highlighted.

5 In the **File and Folder Tasks** box, click on **Rename this file** (Figure 1.36).

6 Press the **Backspace** key to delete the existing name.

7 Enter the new filename (Figure 1.37).

8 Press the **Enter** key.

9 The file is renamed.

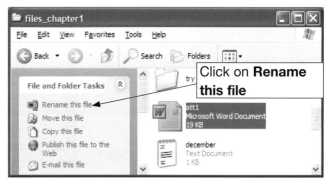

FIGURE 1.36 Renaming a file

FIGURE 1.37 Typing the new filename

Check your understanding *Rename a file*

1 In your user area, double-click on the folder **files_chapter1** to open it.

2 The folder opens.

3 Find the file called **att1**.

4 Rename this file **attempt1**.

5 Remain in your user area.

Renaming folders and subfolders

You may want to change the name of an existing folder or subfolder.

rename a folder or subfolder

1 In the **My Computer** window, in your user area, click on the folder to be renamed.

2 The folder is highlighted (usually blue).

3 In the **File and Folder Tasks** box, click on **Rename this folder** (Figure 1.38).

4 Press the **Backspace** key to delete the existing name.

5 Enter the new folder name (Figure 1.39).

6 Press the **Enter** key.

7 The folder is renamed.

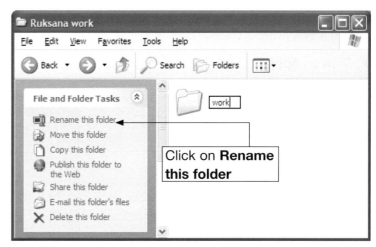

FIGURE 1.38 Renaming a folder

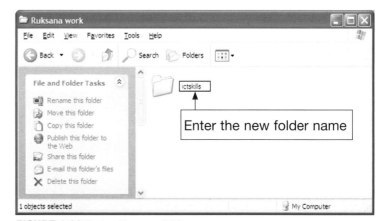

FIGURE 1.39 Typing the new folder name

Check your understanding *Rename a folder*

1 In your user area, rename the folder **work** to **ictskills**.

2 Remain in your user area.

Deleting files and folders

▶▶ How to... *delete a file*

1 In the **My Computer** window, in your user area, double-click on the folder containing the file to be deleted.

2 The folder opens.

3 Click on the file to be deleted.

4 The file is highlighted.

5 In the **File and Folder Tasks** box, click on **Delete this file** (Figure 1.40).

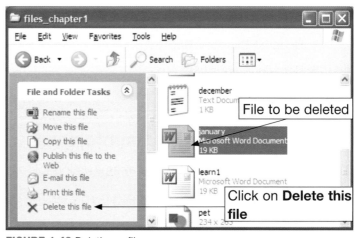

FIGURE 1.40 Deleting a file

6 A **Confirm File Delete** dialogue box is displayed (Figure 1.41).

7 Click on **Yes**. The file is deleted.

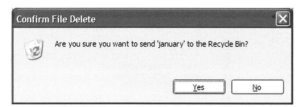

FIGURE 1.41 Confirm File Delete dialogue box

▶▶ *How to...* *delete a folder*

1 In the **My Computer** window, in your user area, click on the folder to be deleted.

2 The folder is highlighted.

3 In the **File and Folder Tasks** box, click on **Delete this folder** (Figure 1.42).

4 A **Confirm Folder Delete** dialogue box is displayed (Figure 1.43).

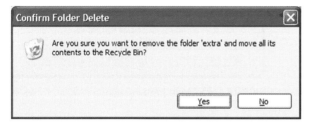

FIGURE 1.43 Confirm Folder Delete dialogue box

5 Click on **Yes**.

6 The folder is deleted.

TIP!

Here's a quick way to delete a file:

1 Click on the file to be deleted.

2 Press the **Delete** key.

3 A **Confirm File Delete** dialogue box is displayed.

4 Click on **Yes**.

TIP!

You can get back any files or folders accidentally deleted by going to the **Recycle Bin**:

1 On the desktop screen, double-click on the **Recycle Bin** icon.

2 Click on the file or folder icon that you had deleted.

3 Click on **Restore**.

4 The file or folder is returned to its original location.

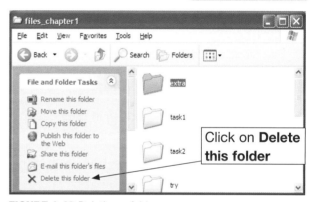

FIGURE 1.42 Deleting a folder

TIP!

Here's a quick way to delete a folder:

1 Click on the folder to be deleted.

2 Press **Delete key**.

3 A **Confirm Folder Delete** dialogue box is displayed.

4 Click on **Yes**.

Check your understanding *Delete a file and a folder*

1 In your user area, open the folder **files_chapter1**.

2 Find and delete the file called **january**.

3 Find and delete the subfolder called **extra**.

4 Remain in your user area.

Moving files and folders

▶▶ How to... *move a file*

1 In the **My Computer** window, in your user area, double-click on the folder containing the file to be moved.

2 The folder opens.

3 Click on the file to be moved.

4 In the **File and Folder Tasks** box, click on **Move this file** (Figure 1.44).

5 A **Move Items** dialogue box is displayed (Figure 1.45).

6 Click on the name of the folder in your user area where the file is to be moved.

7 Click on **Move**.

8 The file is moved to the new location.

▶▶ How to... *move a folder*

1 In the **My Computer** window, in your user area, click on the folder to be moved.

2 In the **File and Folder Tasks** box, click on **Move this folder** (Figure 1.46).

3 A **Move Items** dialogue box is displayed.

4 Click on the name of the place where the folder is to be moved to.

5 Click on **Move**.

6 The folder is moved to the new location.

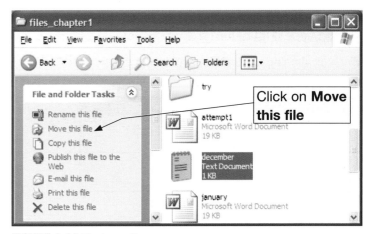

FIGURE 1.44 Moving a file

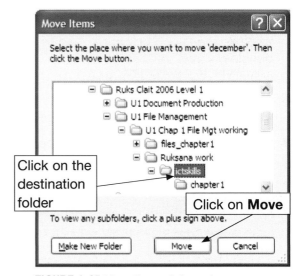

FIGURE 1.45 Move Items dialogue box

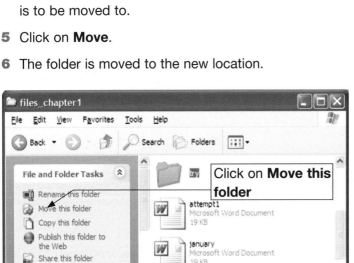

FIGURE 1.46 Moving a folder

1 In your user area, move the file **december** from the folder **files_chapter1** into the folder **ictskills**.

2 Move the folder **try** from the folder **files_chapter1** into the subfolder **chapter1** (the **chapter1** folder is inside the **ictskills** folder).

3 Remain in your user area.

Copying files

▶▶ How to... *copy a file*

1 In the **My Computer** window, in your user area, double-click on the folder containing the file to be copied. The folder contents will be displayed.

2 Click on the file you want to copy.

3 The file is highlighted.

4 In the **File and Folder Tasks** box, click on **Copy this file** (Figure 1.47).

5 A **Copy Items** dialogue box is displayed.

6 Click on the folder name in your user area where the file is to be copied (Figure 1.48).

7 Click on **Copy**.

8 The file is copied into the new folder.

FIGURE 1.47 Copying a file

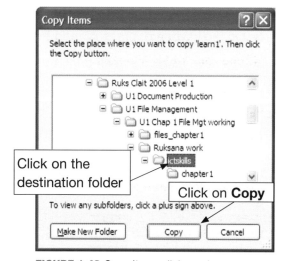

FIGURE 1.48 Copy Items dialogue box

1 In your user area, find the file **learn1** which is in the folder **files_chapter1**.

2 Copy the file **learn1** into the folder **ictskills** (you had renamed the folder **work** to become **ictskills**).

3 Remain in your user area.

Taking screen prints

Find the **Print Screen** key on your keyboard (Figure 1.49). This may be displayed as **Print Screen** or **Prt SC** or **Prnt Scrn** or similar. Now, find the **Alt** key on your keyboard.

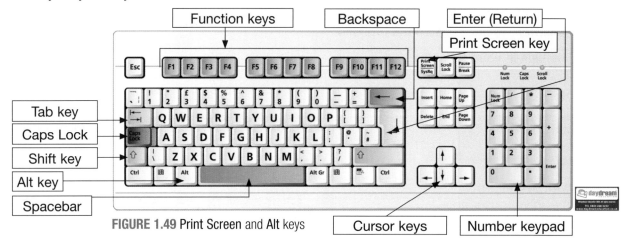

FIGURE 1.49 Print Screen and Alt keys

▶▶ How to... *take a screen print to show the contents of a folder*

1 From the **My Computer** window, go to your user area.

2 To open the folder that you want to take a screen print of, double-click on it.

3 On the keyboard, press **Alt** and **Print Screen** at the same time.

4 You have taken a screen print, but you will not see anything change on your screen.

5 Next, you will need to paste the screen print into a Word document.

6 Open a blank Word document. (If you need reminding how to open a Microsoft Word document, see page 19.)

7 In the document, enter your **name** and **centre number**.

8 Press **Enter**.

9 Click on the **Paste** icon.

10 The screen print is pasted into the Word document.

11 Now you will need to save the screen print.

▶▶ How to... *save the screen print*

1 In your Word document, click on the **File** menu.

2 The **File** menu is displayed.

3 Click on **Save** (Figure 1.50).

> **TIP!**
>
> If you press **Print Screen** only, this takes a screenshot of the whole screen instead of just the window.

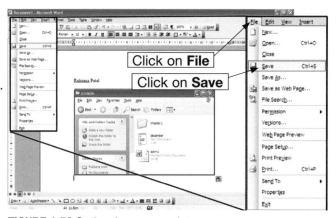

Click on **File**

Click on **Save**

FIGURE 1.50 Saving the screen print

4 A **Save As** dialogue box is displayed (Figure 1.51).

5 Click on the **down arrow** to the right of the **Save in** box, then click on your user area.

6 Double-click to open the folder(s) in your user area, locate your working folder.

7 In the **File name** box, delete any text (e.g. your name).

8 Then enter the required filename into the box (Figure 1.52).

9 Click on **Save**.

10 The screen print is saved in your user area and the **Save As** dialogue box closes.

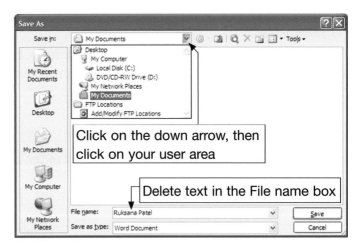

> Click on the down arrow, then click on your user area

> Delete text in the File name box

FIGURE 1.51 Save As dialogue box

▶▶ How to... *print a screen print*

1 In your Word document, click on the **Print** icon on the toolbar.

2 Your screen print will be printed.

3 To close the document, click on the red **Close** ✕ icon on the top right of the window. You will be returned to your user area.

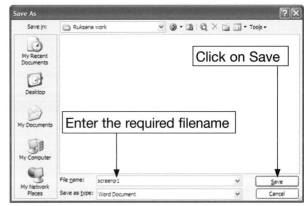

> Click on Save

> Enter the required filename

FIGURE 1.52 Enter the required filename

Check your understanding *Take a screen print of your folder*

1 In your user area, open the folder **ictskills**.

2 Take a screen print of the contents of this folder.

3 Open a new Word document.

4 Enter your name in this document.

5 Paste the screen print into the Word document.

6 Save the Word document in your user area using the filename **screenp1**.

7 Print the file **screenp1**.

8 Close the file **screenp1** and exit Word.

9 Your screen print should display the contents of the **ictskills** folder as shown in Figure 1.53.

10 Remain in your user area.

FIGURE 1.53 Your screen print of the **ictskills** folder should look similar to this

▶▶ How to... *take a screen print of a subfolder*

Repeat all the guidelines in *How to... take a screen print to show the contents of a folder*, *How to... print a screen print*, and *How to... save a screen print*.

▶▶ How to... *close the My Computer window*

○ Click on the Close ☒ icon at the top right of the **My Computer** window.

Check your understanding *Take a screen print of a subfolder*

1 In your user area, open the subfolder **chapter1** (which is in the **ictskills** folder).

2 Take a screen print of the contents of this folder.

3 Open a new Word document.

4 Enter your **name** and **centre number** in this document.

5 Paste the screen print into the document.

6 Save the Word document into your user area using the filename **screenp2**.

7 Print the file **screenp2**.

8 Close the file **screenp2** and exit Word.

9 Your screen print should display the contents of the **chapter1** subfolder as shown in Figure 1.54.

FIGURE 1.54 Your screen print of the **chapter1** subfolder should look similar to this

10 Close the **My Computer** window.

ASSESS YOUR SKILLS – File management

By working through Section 2 you will have learnt the skills below. Read each item to help you decide how confident you feel about each skill.

- recognise file and folder icons

- create and name a folder

- create and name a subfolder

- change the display so that file extensions are not displayed (optional)

- rename a file

- rename a folder

- delete a file

- delete a folder

- move a file

- copy a file

- take a screen print to display the contents of folders

- start Word (and enter text)

- paste a screen print into Word

- save a screen print

- print a screen print

- close and exit Word

- close the **My Computer** window.

If you think you need more practice on any of the skills above, go back and work through the skill(s) again.

If you feel confident, move on to Chapter 2. You may wish to work through Build-up task 1 – File management now.

In the second part of Unit 1, you will produce a word-processed document and make changes to a document that is provided.

You will use a software program, **Microsoft Office Word 2003**, which is part of Microsoft Office and which will help you to create, format and update documents easily. We will refer to it as Word from now on.

This chapter is divided into two sections:

- *in Section 1, you will learn how to create a new document*

- *in Section 2, you will learn how to edit (make changes to) a document.*

How to work through this chapter

1 Before you begin this chapter, make sure that you feel confident with the skills covered in Chapter 1.

2 Read the explanation of a term first.

3 If there are some terms you do not understand, refer to Unit 1 Definition of terms on page 114.

4 Work through the chapter in sequence so that one skill is understood before moving on to the next. This ensures understanding of the topic and prevents unnecessary mistakes.

5 Read the ▶▶ *How to...* guidelines which give step-by-step instructions for each skill. Do not attempt to work through the How to... guidelines, read through each point and look at the screenshots. Make sure you understand all the instructions before moving on.

6 To make sure that you have understood how to perform a skill, work through the Check your understanding task following that skill. You should refer to the How to... instructions when doing the task.

7 At the end of each section, there is an Assess your skills table. This lists the skills that you will have practised by working through each section. Look at each item listed to help you decide whether you are confident that you can perform each skill.

8 Towards the end of the chapter are Quick reference guides, Build-up and Practice tasks. Work through each of the tasks.

If you need help, you may refer to the How to... guidelines or Quick reference guides whilst doing the Build-up tasks. Whilst working on the Practice task, you should feel confident enough to use only the Quick reference guides if you need support. These guides may also be used during an assessment.

A CD-ROM accompanies this book. On it are the files that you will need to use for the tasks for editing a document. Instructions for copying the files are provided at the beginning of Chapter 2 Section 2 on page 74. The solutions for all the tasks can be found in a folder called **worked_copies_unit1**.

Note: there are many ways of performing the skills covered in this book. This book provides How to... guidelines that are easily understood by learners.

1: Create a new document

LEARNING OUTCOMES

In this section you will learn how to:

- start Word
- identify the different parts of Word
- set the page orientation
- set the margins
- set the line spacing
- enter text, numbers and symbols
- save a new document
- set the text alignment
- set the font size
- set the font type
- use spell check
- save an existing document
- use the **Show/Hide** tool
- print a document
- use headers and footers
- use automatic fields in headers/footers
- close a document and exit Word.

Preparing your work area

Now that you have learned to create folders and subfolders, it is advisable to prepare your user area so that you can keep your files organised.

An example of a folder structure for all units is shown in Figure 1.59. The main folder in **My Documents** is called **Ruks Clait 2006 Level 1**. Within this folder are subfolders for each of the units.

You may not need to create as many folders or you may prefer to create a folder for a unit when you begin a new unit or a new chapter.

For Unit 1, two subfolders have been created – one for Chapter 1 File management and another for Chapter 2 Document production.

Within each unit subfolder, there are further subfolders.

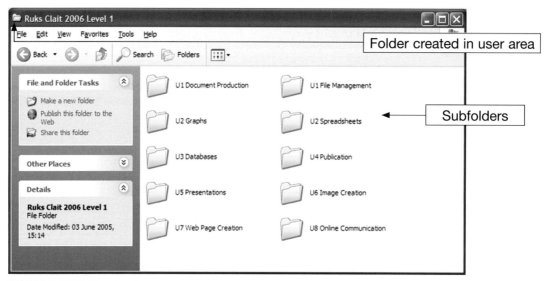

FIGURE 1.59 Folder structure

For example in the **U1 Document Production** subfolder, the four subfolders are:

- **U1 Chap 2 WP working** – *this is the working folder in which all files will be saved*
- **files_chapter2** – *the source files from the CD-ROM have been copied into this folder*
- **worked_copies_unit1** – *this folder has also been copied from the CD-ROM*
- **Copy of files_chapter2** – *this comprises a copy of the folder containing the source files.*

These subfolders are shown in Figure 1.60.

FIGURE 1.60 Subfolders in the **U1 Document Production** subfolder

What is word processing?

Word processing is using a computer to create and edit documents. To perform word processing, you need a computer and a word processing program such as Microsoft Word.

Word processing enables you to create a document, save it, display it on a screen, make changes to it and print it.

The advantage of word processing is that you can make changes to a document as many times as you want without retyping the entire document. You can correct, delete, insert, move and format text very easily. When you have made all the changes you want, you can print the file.

A document appears on the screen exactly as it will look when printed – this is known as WYSIWYG (What You See Is What You Get).

You will learn various word processing skills and techniques as you work through this chapter.

Word processing terms and actions will be explained throughout the chapter.

To remind yourself of the different mouse techniques, see Chapter 1, page 13.

Now, using the skills you learned in Chapter 1, switch on your computer and log in.

What does it mean?

User area
A user area is the workspace on a computer where you save your files.

Starting Word

1 On the desktop screen, click on **Start**.

2 The **Windows XP Start** menu is displayed (Figure 1.61).

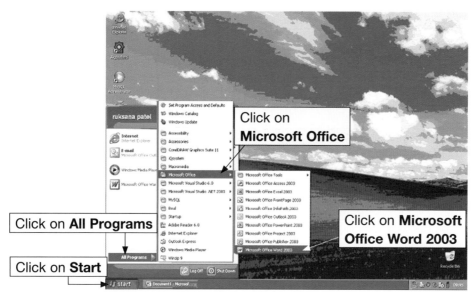

FIGURE 1.61 Starting Microsoft Office Word 2003

3 Click on **All Programs**.

4 The **All Programs** menu appears.

5 Click on **Microsoft Office**.

6 A list of Microsoft Office programs is displayed.

7 Click on **Microsoft Office Word 2003**.

8 A blank Microsoft Word document is displayed.

A quicker way to start Word is to double-click on the Word icon on the desktop (if a shortcut has been created) or to single-click on the Word icon on the **Taskbar** (if a shortcut has been created) (Figure 1.62).

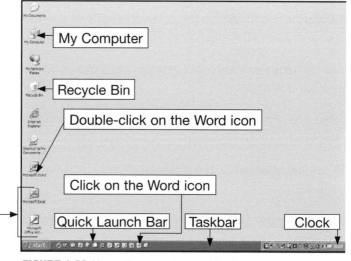

FIGURE 1.62 Alternative ways to start Word

1 Open Word, either through the Start menu or by using a shortcut icon.

2 A new blank document called **Document1** is displayed.

3 Keep this document open.

Getting familiar with the Word window

Word 2003 may open with the **Task Pane** on the right (Figure 1.63). Click on the black cross to close the **Task Pane**.

Take a few minutes to learn about the different parts of the Word window (Figure 1.64).

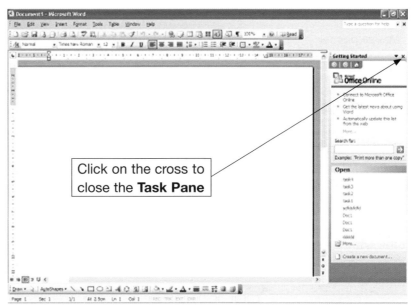

Click on the cross to close the **Task Pane**

FIGURE 1.63 The Task Pane

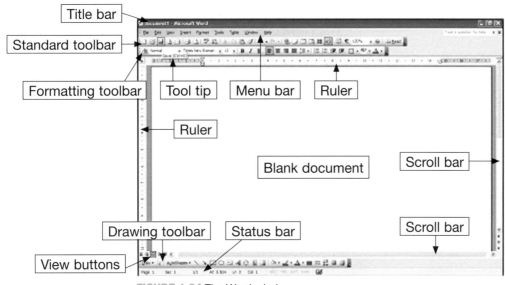

Title bar

Standard toolbar

Formatting toolbar   Tool tip   Menu bar   Ruler

Ruler

Blank document   Scroll bar

Drawing toolbar   Status bar   Scroll bar

View buttons

FIGURE 1.64 The Word window

PART OF WINDOW	DESCRIPTION
Title bar	Displays the title of the current document
Menu bar	A list of options; click on a menu item to see the drop-down menu
Ruler	Vertical and horizontal rulers can be displayed to help you view the page
Standard toolbar	Includes icons for commonly used tasks, e.g. save, print
Formatting toolbar	Includes icons for commonly used formatting, e.g. bold, centre
Tool tip	When the mouse is hovered on a toolbar button, a Tool tip displays showing the name of the button
Blank document	The main document window, where text is entered
Cursor	The position where text will be entered
Mouse pointer	Displays the position of the mouse on screen
Scroll bar	Allows you to scroll up/down or left/right to view the document
View buttons	Different ways of viewing the Word screen. The view in Figure 1.64 is Print Layout View which displays the page centrally with both scroll bars
Drawing toolbar	Includes icons for common drawing items, e.g. text box, arrow
Status bar	Displays the status of the current document, e.g. number of pages, current page, line

The Word window

Getting familiar with Word

If the **Office Assistant** icon is visible in a Word document, right-click on it. A menu is displayed. Click on **Hide** to remove the Office Assistant from the screen.

▶▶ How to... *use Word menus*

1 In your Word document, look for the **Menu bar** (Figure 1.65).

2 Click on **File**.

3 A menu (list) drops down with further choices (Figure 1.66).

4 At first, the whole menu may not display, but if you leave it open for a few seconds it displays in full.

5 Another way to display the full menu is to click on the chevrons ⟱ button at the bottom of the menu as soon as the menu drops down.

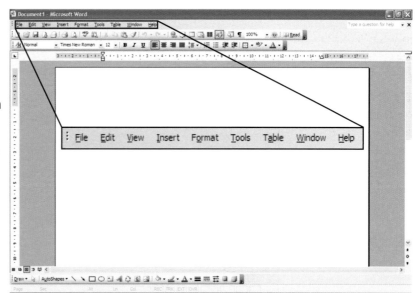

FIGURE 1.65 The **Menu bar**

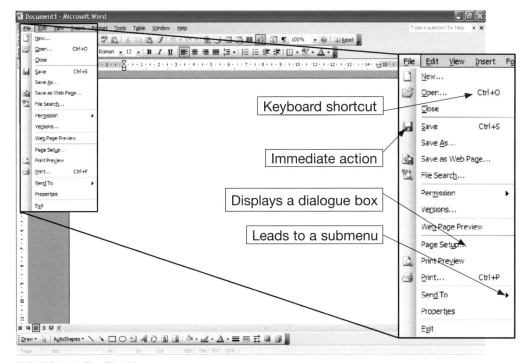

Labels on the figure:
- Keyboard shortcut
- Immediate action
- Displays a dialogue box
- Leads to a submenu

FIGURE 1.66 The **File** Menu

6 Click in the white area of your document (away from the menu) or click on **File** in the **Menu bar** to close the menu.

7 Click on the **Edit** menu.

8 Notice how some options are **ghosted** (paler grey) (Figure 1.67). This means that these options are not available at the moment.

9 Close the **Edit** menu.

The Toolbar buttons

In your Word document, move the mouse over each **Toolbar** button and pause; a **Tool tip** displays, showing the name of the button. In this book, we will refer to a **Toolbar** button as an icon.

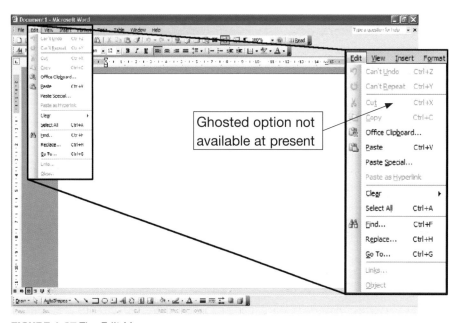

Label on the figure:
- Ghosted option not available at present

FIGURE 1.67 The **Edit** Menu

Making the Word window clearer

The Task Pane

Word 2003 opens with the **Task Pane** on the right of the screen (Figure 1.68). You are advised to close the **Task Pane** so that the screen is clearer (optional).

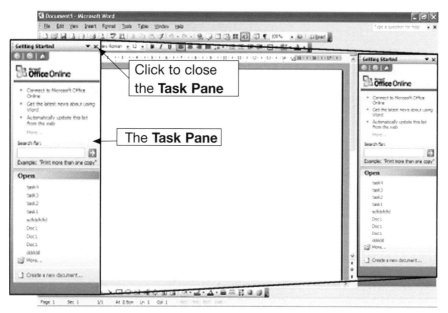

Click to close the **Task Pane**

The **Task Pane**

FIGURE 1.68 Closing the Task Pane

You can either click on the black cross just above the **Task Pane** to close it every time you start Word, or set the option to close the **Task Pane** so that it does not display every time you start Word.

▶▶ How to... *set the option to close the Task Pane (optional)*

1 In your Word document, click on **Tools** (Figure 1.69).

2 From the **Tools** menu, click on **Options**.

3 The **Options** dialogue box is displayed.

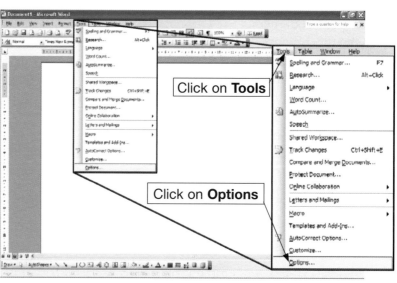

Click on **Tools**

Click on **Options**

FIGURE 1.69 The Tools menu

4 Click on the **View** tab to select it
   (Figure 1.70).

5 Click in the **Startup Task Pane** box to
   remove the tick.

6 Click on **OK**.

7 The **Task Pane** will no longer display every
   time you start Word.

Standard and Formatting toolbars

Look at your Word document. Are the **Standard**
and **Formatting toolbars** on the same row as
shown in Figure 1.71?

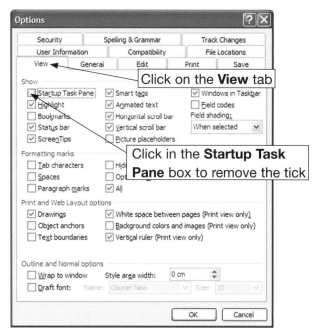

FIGURE 1.70 Options dialogue box with View option
selected

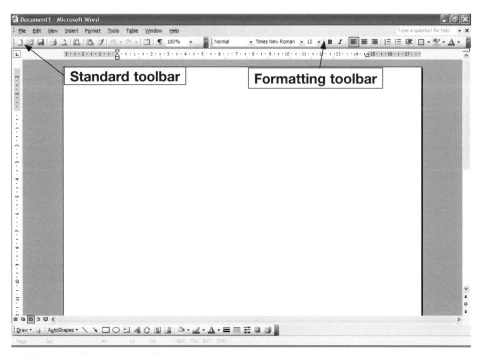

FIGURE 1.71 Standard and Formatting toolbars on the same row

If so, it is helpful to display them on two rows so that you can see all the
icons on both toolbars

> **▶▶ How to...**   *display the Standard and Formatting*
> *toolbars on two rows (optional)*

1 In your Word document, click on the **Toolbar Options** ▤ symbol at the
   right end of the **Standard toolbar**.

2 A menu is displayed (Figure 1.72).

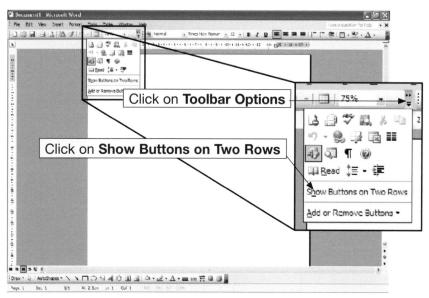

Click on **Toolbar Options**

Click on **Show Buttons on Two Rows**

FIGURE 1.72 More buttons menu

3 Click on **Show Buttons on Two Rows**.

4 The **Standard** and **Formatting toolbars** will now display on two rows (Figure 1.73).

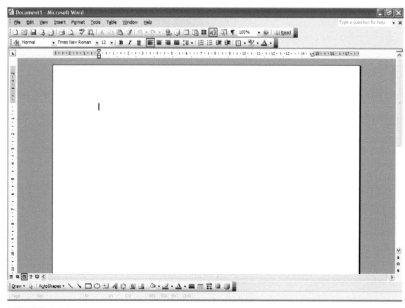

FIGURE 1.73 Standard and Formatting toolbars on separate rows

Page orientation

▶▶ How to... *set the page orientation*

1 In the **Menu bar**, click on **File**.

2 From the **File** menu, click on **Page Setup**.

3 The **Page Setup** dialogue box is displayed.

4 Select the **Margins** tab.

5 Click on **Portrait** or **Landscape** (Figure 1.74).

6 Click on **OK**.

7 The page will either be displayed portrait or landscape.

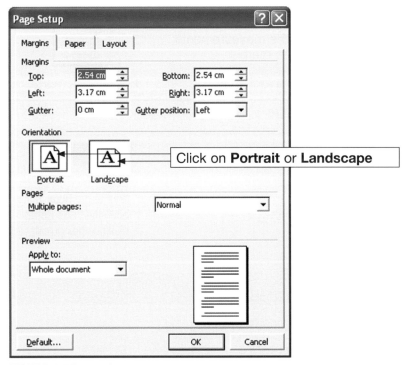

FIGURE 1.74 **Page Setup** dialogue box

What does it mean?

Page orientation
Page orientation refers to which way round the paper is displayed:
- **Portrait** – an A4 sheet of paper displayed with the shortest sides at the top and bottom.
- **Landscape** – an A4 sheet displayed with the longest sides at the top and bottom.

Check your understanding *Set the page orientation*

A blank document called Document1 should open when you start Word.

1 In Document1, set the page orientation to portrait.

Margins

Margins are the amount of white space from the edge of the paper to the text on the page. In Word you can set the top, bottom, left and right margins.

▶▶ How to... *set margins*

1 In the **Menu bar**, click on **File**.

2 From the **File** menu, click on **Page Setup**.

3 The **Page Setup** dialogue box is displayed.

4 Check that the **Margins** tab is selected.

5 Click in the box for **Top**, enter the measurements for the top margin, then do the same for the **Left**, **Right** and **Bottom** margins (Figure 1.75).

6 You can use the **up/down arrows**; however, this may not allow you to set margins to specific measurements.

7 You do not need to enter **cm** (centimetres) into the measurements box, as Word will do this automatically.

8 Click on **OK** to set the margins.

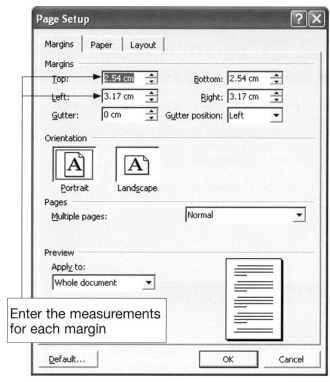

Enter the measurements for each margin

FIGURE 1.75 Setting the margins

TIP!

Double-click on the blue area of the **Ruler bar** to open the **Page Setup** dialogue box quickly.

Check your understanding *Set the margins*

1 In **Document1**, set the top, left and right margins to **3.3 cm**.

2 Do not change the bottom margin measurement.

Line spacing

Line spacing is the amount of space between each line of text. Line spacing can be set before entering text; if so, the line spacing set will be applied to all the text. Line spacing can also be set after entering text to all or part of a document.

 **How to...** *set the line spacing*

1 Click on the **Format** menu.

2 From the menu, click on **Paragraph**.

3 The **Paragraph** dialogue box is displayed (Figure 1.76).

4 Select the **Indents and Spacing** tab.

5 Under **Line spacing** click on the **down arrow**.

6 Click on the line spacing option required, e.g. **Single**.

7 Click on **OK** to set the line spacing.

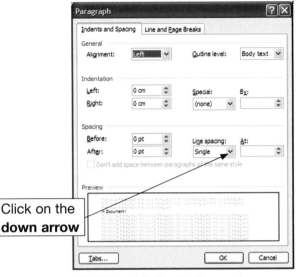

Click on the **down arrow**

FIGURE 1.76 Setting the line spacing

Check your understanding *Set the line spacing*

In **Document1**, set the line spacing to **single**.

Entering text, numbers and symbols

Entering text is also referred to as typing or keying in text. When you enter text, make sure you **enter the words exactly** as shown.

Use the **same case** as shown in the text you are copying:

○ *this text is in **lower case** – there are no capital letters*

○ *Each Of These Words Has An **Initial Capital** – The First Letter Of Each Word Is A Capital*

○ *THIS TEXT IS IN **UPPERCASE** – ALL THE LETTERS ARE CAPITAL LETTERS.*

When you enter text, make sure you use the **correct spacing**.

WHERE	NUMBER OF SPACES
Between each word	One space
After a comma	One space
After a full stop	Two spaces (one space is also commonly used)
After a colon	One space
After a semicolon	One space
Between paragraphs	One clear line space between each paragraph

Spacing in text

To remind yourself of the keyboard and How to... Use the keyboard, see Chapter 1, page 17.

Points to remember when entering text

- *Use the same case as shown.*
- *Use the correct spacing between words and after punctuation.*
- *Do not press the **Enter** key at the end of a line within a paragraph.*
- *Press the **Enter** key twice after a heading.*
- *Press the **Enter** key twice at the end of a paragraph.*

What does it mean?

Word wrap
A word that is too long to fit on the end of a line is automatically placed on the next line. This breaks lines automatically between words, so that when the text being entered on the line reaches beyond the right-hand margin, the whole of the last word is transferred to the beginning of the next line.

Check your understanding *Enter text*

1 In **Document1**, enter the text below.

2 Do not worry if you make any spelling or spacing errors, you will learn to correct these later.

3 Refer to the table, Using the keyboard, in Chapter 1, page 17, if you need to.

LEARNING NEW SKILLS

I am learning how to produce a document using Microsoft Word. To help with my typing skills I have been told to type the following sentence which contains all the letters of the alphabet: The quick brown fox jumps over the lazy dog.

Soon I will be able to write letters to friends, relatives and colleagues using the skills I have learned.

Saving a Word document

A document must be saved if you want to use it again. It is good practice to save your work approximately every 10 minutes so that you do not lose too much work if there is a computer problem. A new document should be given an appropriate filename when saving for the first time; after that it can be saved keeping the same filename or with a new filename.

▶▶ How to... *save a Word document into a new folder*

1 In the **Menu bar**, click on **File**.

2 From the **File** menu, click on **Save**.

3 A **Save As** dialogue box is displayed.

4 Click on the **down arrow** to the right of the **Save in** box, then click on your user area (Figure 1.77). You may need to double-click to open any sub-folders in your user area.

5 Click on the **Create New Folder** icon.

TIP!

It is good practice to keep your saved files organised in folders.

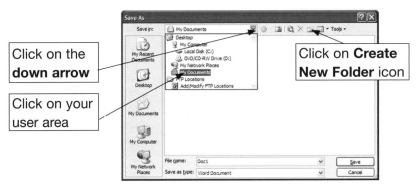

Click on the **down arrow**

Click on your user area

Click on **Create New Folder** icon

FIGURE 1.77 **Save As** dialogue box

FIGURE 1.78 **New Folder** dialogue box

6 A **New Folder** dialogue box is displayed (Figure 1.78).

7 Enter the new folder name.

8 Click on **OK.**

9 In the **Save As** dialogue box, delete any existing text in the **File name** box.

10 Enter the required filename (Figure 1.79).

11 Click on **Save**.

12 Your document is saved in a new folder within your user area.

Enter the new filename

FIGURE 1.79 Entering the required filename in the **Save As** dialogue box

Check your understanding
Save your document into a new folder

Save **Document1** into a new folder called **ocrunit1** using the filename **practice1**.

Text alignment

Before learning how to set the text alignment, you will need to know how to highlight text in a document.

TEXT	HOW TO HIGHLIGHT
A word	Position the mouse pointer over the word and **double-click.**
A phrase (a few words)	Position the mouse pointer just before the first word in the phrase and click, hold down the **Shift** key on the keyboard, position the mouse pointer just after the last word of the phrase and click.
A sentence	Hold down the **Ctrl** key on the keyboard and click anywhere in the sentence.
A paragraph	Position the mouse pointer anywhere in the paragraph and triple-click (click three times very quickly).
The whole document	Press the **Ctrl** and **A** keys at the same time.

Methods of highlighting text in a document

Left-aligned text has a neat left-hand edge and a ragged right-hand edge as displayed in the text you are reading. Words are equally spaced.

Right-aligned text has a neat right-hand edge and a ragged left-hand edge as displayed in the text you are reading. Words are equally spaced.

Justified text (also sometimes called fully justified) has straight edges on both sides as displayed in the text you are reading. Wider spaces may appear between words.

Centred text is positioned centrally between the left and right margins or within each table cell as displayed in the text you are reading.

What does it mean?

Alignment
Alignment is how the text lines up with the left and right margins. In word processing, you can align text to the **left**, **centre**, **right**, or on both the left and right (referred to as **justified** text).

▶▶ How to... *set the text alignment*

Text alignment can be set before or after you enter text.

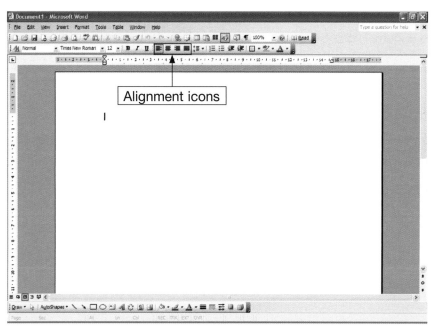

FIGURE 1.80 Alignment icons in the **Formatting** toolbar

Before you enter text

To left-align text:

○ *click on the **Align Left*** 🔲 *icon in the **Formatting toolbar**. All the text entered will be left-aligned.*

To right-align text:

○ *click on the **Align Right*** 🔲 *icon in the **Formatting toolbar**. All the text entered will be right-aligned.*

To justify text:

○ *click on the **Justify*** 🔲 *icon in the **Formatting toolbar**. All the text entered will be aligned to the left and to the right.*

Note: wider spaces may appear within sentences in justified text.

To centre text:

○ *click the **Center*** ☰ *icon in the **Formatting toolbar**. All the text entered will be centred.*

After you enter text

Highlight the text to be aligned and click the left, right, centre or justify icon.

Saving an existing document

Remember to save your document **practice1** approximately every 10 minutes. Saving an existing document that you have previously saved and named is quicker than saving a new document for the first time.

▶▶ **How to...** *save an existing document*

1 In the **Menu bar**, click on **File**.

2 From the **File** menu, click on **Save**.

TIP!

Click on the **Save** 💾 icon *OR* press **Ctrl** and **S** keys at the same time.

Check your understanding   *Set the text alignment*

1 Refer to the 'Methods of highlighting text in a document' on page 57.

2 Apply the following alignments to the text in the document **practice1**:

  a **Centre** the heading LEARNING NEW SKILLS.

  b **Justify** all the text in the first paragraph.

  c **Right-align** all the text in the second paragraph.

3 Save your document keeping the filename **practice1**.

Font size

Font size refers to the height of the characters (letters, numbers, symbols). A small font size will display small characters and a large font size displays large characters. Examples of font sizes:

Font size 10

Font size 12

Font size 14.

▶▶ **How to...** *set the font size*

Font size can be set before or after you enter text.

Before you enter text

1 In the **Formatting toolbar**, select the required font size by clicking on the **drop-down arrow** to the right of the **Font Size** box (Figure 1.81).

2 A list of sizes is displayed.

3 Click on the required size. All text that you enter will be in the font size that you selected.

After you enter text

1 Highlight the text to be changed.

2 In the **Formatting toolbar**, select the required font size by clicking on the **drop-down arrow** to the right of the **Font Size** box.

3 A list of sizes is displayed.

4 Click on the required size.

5 The font size of the highlighted text will change.

6 Click anywhere in your document to remove the highlight from the selected text (to deselect the text).

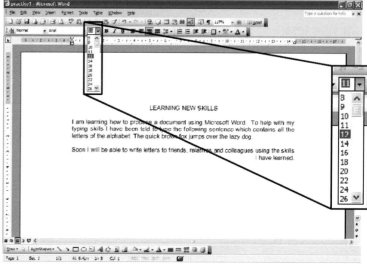

FIGURE 1.81 Setting the font size

Check your understanding
Change the font size of existing text

In the document **practice1**:

1 Highlight the heading and set it to **font size 14.**

2 Highlight the first paragraph and set it to **font size 12.**

3 Highlight the second paragraph and set it to **font size 10.**

4 Save the document keeping the filename **practice1.**

Check your understanding
Set the font size and alignment before entering new text

1 In the document **practice1**, place your cursor at the end of the second paragraph and create a new paragraph by pressing **Enter** twice.

2 Set the **font size** to **11**.

3 Set the **text alignment** to **left**.

4 Enter the following text as the third paragraph:

Another good sentence to practise keyboarding is: Now is the time for all good men to come to the aid of the party.

5 Save the document keeping the filename **practice1.**

Font type

Font type refers to the font name. It is also referred to as font or font style. Examples of font types are Arial, Times New Roman, Comic Sans MS.

▶▶ How to... *set the font type*

The font type can be set before or after you enter text.

Before you enter text

1 In the **Formatting toolbar**, click on the **drop-down arrow** to the right of the **Font** box, where the font name is displayed (Figure 1.82).

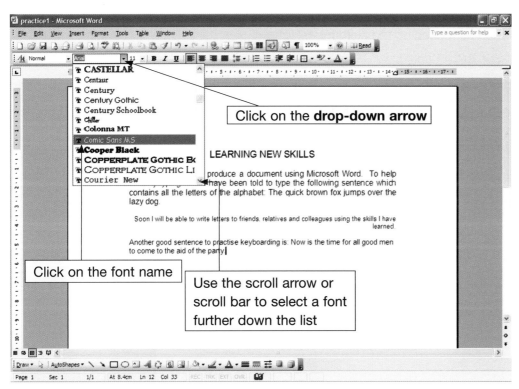

FIGURE 1.82 Setting the font type

2 A list of available fonts is displayed.

3 Click on the required font name from the list. All text that you enter will be in the font type that you selected.

After you enter text

1 Highlight the text you want to change.

2 Click on the **drop-down arrow** to the right of the **Font** box, where the font name is displayed.

3 A list of available fonts is displayed.

TIP!

The available fonts are listed in alphabetical order. To choose a font that is not visible, use the scroll bar or scroll arrow to find a font that is further down the list, or enter the first letter of the font name.

4 Click on the required font name from the list.

5 The font type of the selected text will change.

6 Click anywhere in your document to deselect the text.

In the document **practice1**:

1 Set the **font type** of the heading to **Times New Roman**.

2 Set the **font type** of the first paragraph to **Arial**.

3 Set the **font type** of the second paragraph to **Comic Sans MS**.

4 Set the **font type** of the third paragraph to **Lucida Handwriting**.

5 Save the document keeping the filename **practice1**.

Your document should now look similar to the one in Figure 1.83.

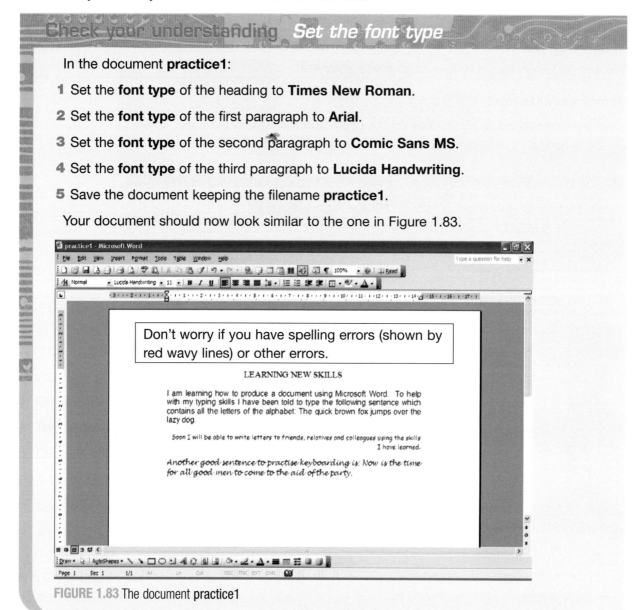

FIGURE 1.83 The document practice1

Checking your document for errors

Always check your work for errors. Even though the spell checker may be set to check your spelling as you type, it cannot check for missing or incorrect words (e.g. come instead of came). Therefore, you must still check the whole document yourself.

It is very important that you spell check using a UK spell checker. Before you start checking for spelling errors, you must check that the language is set to **English (U.K.)**.

1 In the **Menu bar**, click on **Tools**.

2 From the **Tools** menu, click on **Language**.

3 From the **Language** menu click on **Set Language**.

4 The **Language** dialogue box is displayed (Figure 1.84).

5 Make sure **English (U.K.)** is highlighted. If it isn't, click on it.

6 Click on **OK**.

How to... *spell check a document*

1 In the **Standard toolbar**, click on the **Spelling and Grammar** icon.

2 Word checks the whole document for spelling errors.

3 If the spell checker finds an error, the **Spelling and Grammar** dialogue box is displayed (Figure 1.85).

4 The incorrect word is highlighted in red in the **Not in Dictionary** box.

5 Alternative spellings are displayed in the **Suggestions** box.

How to... *change the spelling of an incorrect word*

If the correct spelling is displayed in the Suggestions box

1 Click on the correct spelling of the word in the **Suggestions** box.

2 Click on **Change**.

3 The spelling will be changed in your document, a dialogue box displays telling you that the spelling and grammar check is complete.

4 Click **OK**.

If the correct spelling is not displayed in the Suggestions box

You will need to know how to spell the word correctly.

1 In the **Spelling and Grammar** dialogue box, highlight the incorrectly spelt word in the **Not in the dictionary** box.

2 Enter the correct spelling of the word.

3 Click on **Change**.

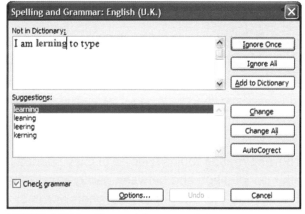

FIGURE 1.84 **Language** dialogue box

FIGURE 1.85 Spelling and Grammar dialogue box

What does it mean?

Spell checker
Word has a **spell checker** tool which automatically checks the spelling in a document against a large dictionary. Word shows possible spelling errors or repeated words with a red wavy line shown under the word. Green wavy lines show possible grammar errors. If you are copy-typing text, you should ignore any alternative grammar suggestions.

4 The spelling will be changed in your document.

5 Click **OK**.

Sometimes Word will highlight a word as being incorrectly spelt, even though it is correct, because that word is not in Word's UK English dictionary (e.g. your name).

▶▶ How to... *ignore a suggested spelling*

1 Make sure that the highlighted word is spelt correctly.

2 In the **Spelling and Grammar** dialogue box, click on **Ignore Once** (if you know the word appears only once in the document) OR **Ignore All** (if you know the word appears more than once in the document).

Check your understanding *Spell check your document*

1 In the document **practice1**, set the language to **English (U.K.)**.

2 Click on the **Spelling and Grammar** icon in the **Standard** toolbar to spell check your document.

3 Correct any spelling errors.

4 Ignore any grammar changes suggested by Word.

The Show/Hide tool

The **Show/Hide** tool is used to display spaces between words, after punctuation and between paragraphs. When you switch on the **Show/Hide** tool each space between words or after punctuation is represented by a dot. A paragraph marker ¶ shows each time that you pressed **Enter**. These dots and markers are referred to as non-printing characters.

Using the **Show/Hide tool** will help you to check a document for accuracy.

▶▶ How to... *switch on the Show/Hide tool*

In the **Standard** toolbar, click on the **Show/Hide** ¶ icon to switch on the **Show/Hide tool**. (To switch it off, click on the icon again.)

TIP!

The dots and markers will not print whether the **Show/Hide** tool is switched on or off when you send the document to print.

Check your understanding
Use the Show/Hide tool to check your document

1 In the document **practice1**, click on the Show/Hide icon.

Your document should look similar to the one in Figure 1.86.

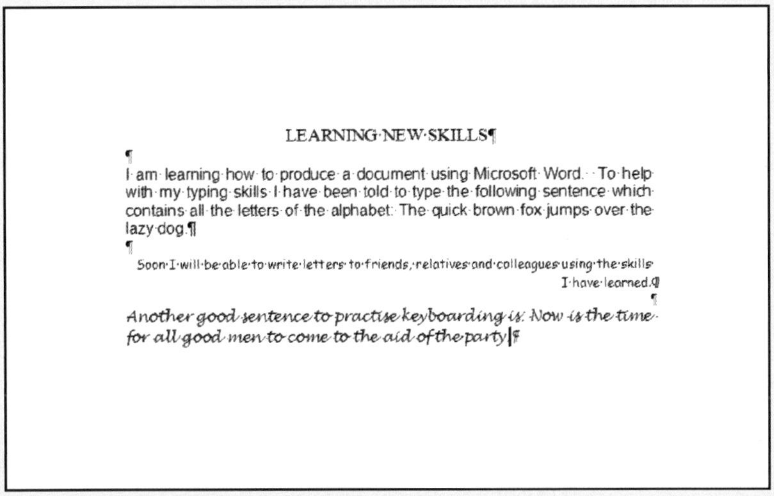

LEARNING·NEW·SKILLS¶

¶

I·am·learning·how·to·produce·a·document·using·Microsoft·Word.··To·help·with·my·typing·skills·I·have·been·told·to·type·the·following·sentence·which·contains·all·the·letters·of·the·alphabet:·The·quick·brown·fox·jumps·over·the·lazy·dog.¶

¶

Soon·I·will·be·able·to·write·letters·to·friends,·relatives·and·colleagues·using·the·skills·I·have·learned.¶

¶

Another·good·sentence·to·practise·keyboarding·is:·Now·is·the·time·for·all·good·men·to·come·to·the·aid·of·the·party¶

FIGURE 1.86 The document **practice1** with the **Show/Hide** tool switched on

2 Check the spacing. There should be:

- **a** **one dot between each word**
- **b** **one dot after a comma**
- **c** **two dots after a full stop**
- **d** **two paragraph markers for each paragraph**, one will be at the end of the text, the second will be on a clear line.

3 Delete any additional dots or paragraph markers by pressing **Backspace** or **Delete**.

4 If required, insert space(s) between words or after punctuation by using the **Spacebar**. Insert additional paragraph markers by pressing **Enter**.

5 Now, click on the **Show/Hide** icon to switch it off and to view your document normally.

6 Save your document keeping the filename **practice1**.

Printing documents

Before printing a document, it is a good idea to check how it will look when printed by using **Print Preview**.

TIP!

Always use **Print Preview** to check your document before printing.

▶▶ *How to...* *open Print Preview*

1 In the **Standard toolbar**, click on the **Print Preview** 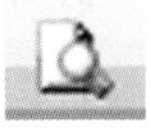 icon.

2 The **Print Preview** window is displayed. Check your document for accuracy.

3 Click on **Close** in the **Print Preview** toolbar to return to your document.

TIP!

Before you print for the first time, check the paper size.

▶▶ How to... *set paper size*

1 In the **Menu bar**, click on **File**.

2 From the **File** menu, click on **Page Setup**.

3 The **Page Setup** dialogue box is displayed.

4 Click on the **Paper** tab to select **Paper** view.

5 Check the **Paper size** box displays **A4**, (Figure 1.87).

6 If not, click on the **drop-down arrow** to the right of the box and click on **A4, 210 x 297mm**.

7 Click on **OK** to confirm the paper size.

▶▶ How to... *print a document*

1 In the **Menu bar**, click on **File**.

2 From the **File** menu, click on **Print** (Figure 1.88).

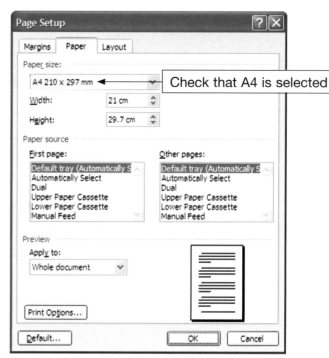

FIGURE 1.87 Page Setup dialogue box in Paper view

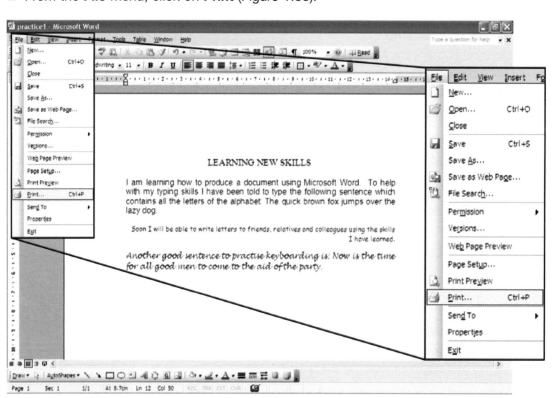

FIGURE 1.88 Click on Print in the File menu

3 A **Print** dialogue box is displayed (Figure 1.89).

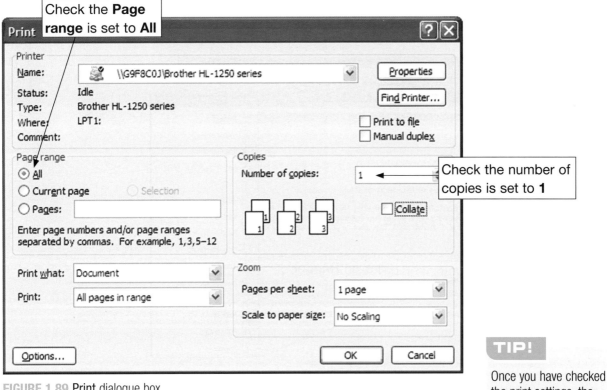

Check the **Page range** is set to **All**

Check the number of copies is set to **1**

FIGURE 1.89 **Print** dialogue box

4 Check that the **Page Range** is set to All.

5 Check that the **Number of copies** box is set to **1**.

6 Click on **OK** to print the document.

Check your understanding *Set paper size and print*

1 In the document **practice1**, check the paper size is **A4**.

2 Print one copy.

Headers and footers

Headers and footers are common identifiers at the top and bottom of a page. They can be displayed on every page or on every other page. Special features such as date, filename and page numbers can be added to a header or footer.

1 In the **Menu bar**, click on **View**.

2 From the View menu, click on **Header and Footer** (Figure 1.90).

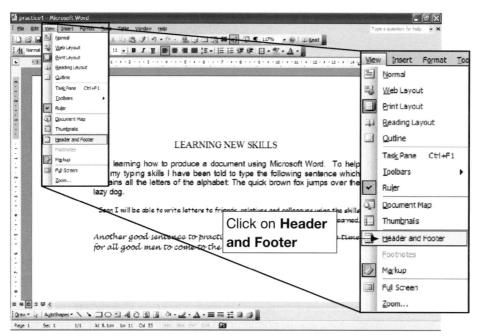

FIGURE 1.90 The **View** menu

3 The cursor is displayed in the header section of the document and the **Header and Footer toolbar** displays on the page (Figure 1.91)

FIGURE 1.91 The Header and Footer toolbar

4 Enter the required information in the header.

5 Click on the **Switch Between Header and Footer** icon to go to the footer section.

6 The cursor is displayed in the footer section of the document.

7 Enter any required information in the footer.

8 Click on **Close** to close the **Header and Footer** toolbar and return to the document.

Automatic fields

Word can insert some information automatically into headers and footers, e.g. automatic dates and automatic filenames. The advantage of using automatic fields is that these will update automatically.

TIP!

If you need to insert several items in the header or footer, e.g. your name, centre number, automatic date and automatic filename, don't click close until you have inserted all items.

TIP!

Check that your computer is set to update fields: click the **Tools** menu, click **Options**, click the **Print** tab, make sure there is a tick in the box for **Update Fields**.

▶▶ How to... add an automatic date

1 Open the **Header and Footer** toolbar.

2 In the header or footer section, click on the **Insert Date** 📅 icon.

3 An automatic date is displayed on the screen.

▶▶ How to... add an automatic filename

1 Open the **Header and Footer** toolbar.

2 In the header or footer section, click on the **drop-down arrow** next to **Insert AutoText**.

3 A drop-down menu is displayed (Figure 1.92).

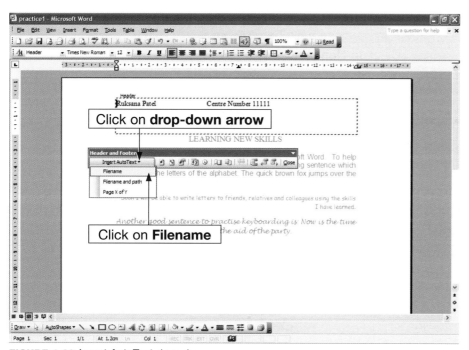

FIGURE 1.92 Insert AutoText drop-down menu

4 Click on **Filename** to automatically insert the document's filename in the header or footer.

5 Click on **Close** to close the **Header and Footer** toolbar and return to the document.

6 Click on the **Print Preview** 🔍 icon to check all headers and footers.

TIP!

When you insert an automatic filename, the saved name may not display immediately; **Document1** may display – this is normal. Use **Print Preview** to check all headers and footers.

TIP!

To make sure that the automatic filename updates after you have saved a document, highlight the filename in the header or footer and press F9.

TIP!

In **Print Layout** view, the headers and footers appear in a lighter shade of grey to the main body text.

TIP!

Remember to save your document again after you have added headers and footers. Click on the **Save** 💾 icon in the **Standard** toolbar.

1 In the document **practice1**, insert the following headers and footers:

 a In the **header**, enter your **first and last name** and your **centre number**.

 b Insert at least **one space** between each item in the header *OR* press the **Tab** key.

 c In the **footer**, insert an **automatic date** and an **automatic filename**.

2 Use **Print Preview** to check your headers and footers.

3 Print one copy of your document.

Closing a document

Now that you have saved and printed your document, you should close it. It is good practice to remember to close a file before you close a program.

▶▶ How to... *close a document*

1 In the **Menu bar**, click on **File**.

2 From the **File** menu, click on **Close** (Figure 1.93).

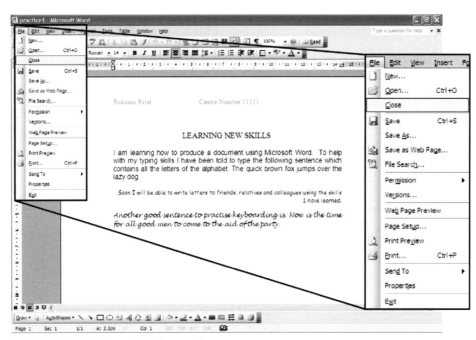

FIGURE 1.93 Closing a Word document

Exiting Word

When the document has been closed, you should exit from Word.

▶▶ How to... *exit from Word*

1 In the **Menu bar**, click on **File**.

2 From the **File** menu, click on **Exit** (Figure 1.94).

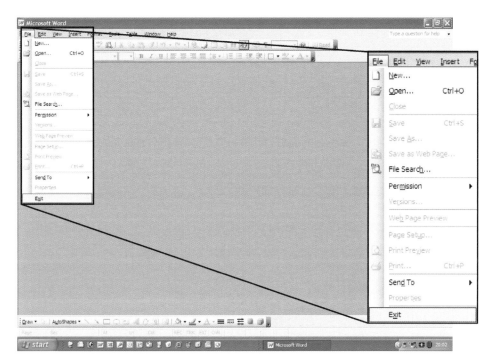

FIGURE 1.94 Exiting Word

TIP!

Once you have saved a document, click on the **Close ☒** icon to close the document and exit Word.

Check your understanding *Close a document and exit Word*

1 Close the document **practice1**.

2 Exit Word.

By working through Section 1 you will have learnt the skills below. Read each item to help you decide how confident you feel about each skill.

- ○ start Word
- ○ understand the different parts of Word
- ○ create a new blank document
- ○ set the page orientation
- ○ set the top, left and right margins
- ○ set the line spacing
- ○ enter text in a blank document
- ○ set the text alignment (left, right, justify and centre)
- ○ set the font size
- ○ set the font type
- ○ use spell check
- ○ use the **Show/Hide** tool
- ○ save a new document with a specified filename
- ○ save a document into a new folder from within Word
- ○ enter text in headers and footers
- ○ insert an automatic date and an automatic filename in headers and footers
- ○ save an updated document keeping the same filename
- ○ print a document
- ○ close a document
- ○ exit Word.

If you think you need more practice on any of the skills listed above, go back and work through the skill(s) again.

If you feel confident, move on to Section 2.

LEARNING OUTCOMES

In this section you will learn how to:

- open a provided document and save it with a different filename
- emphasise text (bold, italic, underline)
- delete text
- move text
- insert text
- use **Find and Replace**
- insert paragraph break
- change line spacing
- use bullets and numbering
- use tabs and indents
- insert a table
- apply borders, gridlines and shading
- use word count.

Useful keyboard shortcuts

To use the keyboard shortcuts shown in the table (left), press both keys at the same time.

Files for this chapter

To work through the tasks in Section 2, you will need the files from the folder called **files_chapter2**, which you will find on the CD-ROM provided with this book. Copy this folder into your user area before you begin.

SHORTCUT KEYS	DESCRIPTION
Ctrl and **B**	Makes highlighted text bold
Ctrl and **I**	Makes highlighted text italic
Ctrl and **U**	Underlines highlighted text
Ctrl and **A**	Highlight the whole document
Ctrl and **C**	Copy the highlighted text
Ctrl and **X**	Cut the highlighted text
Ctrl and **V**	Paste text
Ctrl and **Z**	Undo the last action
Ctrl and **Y**	Redo the last action
Ctrl and **2**	Apply double line spacing to highlighted text
Ctrl and **1**	Apply single line spacing to highlighted text

Keyboard shortcuts

Make sure the computer is switched on and the desktop screen is displayed.

1 Insert the CD-ROM into the CD-ROM drive of your computer.

2 Close any windows that may open.

3 In the desktop, double-click on the **My Computer** icon. The **My Computer** window is displayed.

4 Under Devices with Removable Storage, double-click on the CD Drive icon to view the contents of the CD-ROM.

5 A window opens displaying the contents of the CD-ROM.

6 Double-click on the folder **L1_Unit1_FM+DP**.

7 Double-click on the folder **Source Files**.

8 Click on the folder **files_chapter2** (Figure 1.95).

9 The folder will be highlighted (usually blue).

10 In the **File and Folder Tasks** box, click on **Copy this folder**.

11 A **Copy Items** dialogue box is displayed (Figure 1.96).

12 Click on the user area where you want to copy the folder **files_chapter2**.

13 Click on **Copy**.

14 The folder **files_chapter2** is copied to your user area.

15 It is advisable to copy and paste a second copy to another folder in your user area as backup.

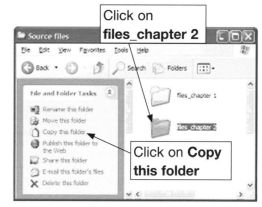

FIGURE 1.95 Source files window

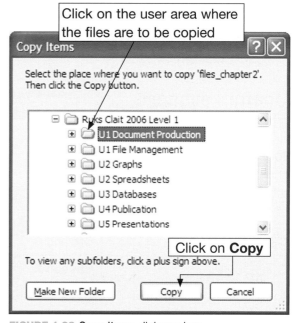

FIGURE 1.96 Copy items dialogue box

 **How to...** *open a provided Word file (1)*

1 In the desktop, double-click on the **My Computer** icon.

2 In the **My Computer** window, double-click on your user area to open it.

3 Double-click on the folder or subfolder containing the required file.

4 The folder contents are displayed.

5 Open the required file by double-clicking on it.

▶▶ How to... *open a provided Word file (2)*

Below is another way to open a Word file.

1 Open a Word document (to remind yourself of the different ways to open Word, see page 46).

2 In the document, click on **File** in the **Menu bar**.

3 From the drop-down **File** menu, click on **Open**.

4 The **Open** dialogue box is displayed.

5 In the **Look in** box, click on the folder or subfolder where the required file is saved.

6 Click on the **down arrow** to the right of the **Look in** box to find the folder if it is not shown in the box. Double-click to open any subfolders.

7 From the files displayed, double-click on the Word file to be opened.

▶▶ How to... *save a file using a new filename in Word 2003 format into an existing folder*

1 In Word, click on **File** in the **Menu bar**.

2 From the **File** menu, click on **Save As**.

3 The **Save As** dialogue box opens (Figure 1.97).

4 Click on the **down arrow** to the right of the **Save in** box and click on the folder where you want to save the file.

5 In the **File name** box, delete the existing filename.

6 Enter the new filename.

7 Click on the **down arrow** to the right of the **Save as type** box.

8 Scroll up to the top of the list and click on **Word Document**.

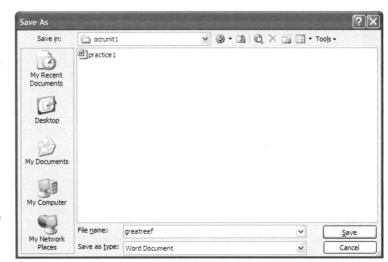

FIGURE 1.97 Save As dialogue box

9 Click on **Save**.

10 The file will be saved with the new filename in Word 2003 format into your folder.

Before you begin, make sure you have copied the folder **files_chapter2** to your user area (see page 74).

1 In your user area, open the file **reef** from the folder **files_chapter2**.

2 Save the file **reef** as a Word 2003 file using the filename **greatreef** into the folder **ocrunit1** that you created earlier.

3 Keep the file open.

Using emphasis

Emphasis is used to make text stand out. Text can be emphasised using **bold**, *italic* or by underlining it.

▶▶ How to... *format the text to be bold*

1 In your document, highlight the text to be made bold.

2 In the **Formatting toolbar**, click on the **Bold** **B** icon. The text is made bold.

3 Click in your document outside the highlighted area to remove the highlight (to deselect the text).

▶▶ How to... *format text into italics*

1 In your document, highlight the text to be italicised.

2 In the **Formatting toolbar**, click on the **Italic** *I* icon. The text is italicised.

3 Click in your document outside the highlighted area to deselect the text.

▶▶ How to... *underline the text*

1 In your document, highlight the text to be underlined.

2 In the **Formatting toolbar**, click on the **Underline** U icon. The text is underlined.

3 Click in your document outside the highlighted area to deselect the text.

1 In the file **greatreef**, format the heading **The Great Barrier Reef** to be **bold**.

2 In the first paragraph, format the text *The Great Barrier Reef* to be **italic**.

3 In the first paragraph, **underline** the text 2000 km.

Deleting text

When you delete text from a document, you remove that text permanently.

▶▶ How to... *delete text*

1 In your document, highlight the text to be deleted. Make sure you also highlight any punctuation after a phrase (comma, full stop, exclamation mark).

2 In the **Formatting toolbar**, click on the **Cut** ✂ icon. The phrase is deleted from the document.

TIP!

A quick way to delete text:

Highlight the text to be deleted, then press the **Delete** key or press **Ctrl** and **X** at the same time.

TIP!

If you accidentally delete text, press **Ctrl** and **Z** at the same time to undo or click the **Undo** icon on the Standard toolbar.

Check your understanding *Delete text*

1 In the file **greatreef**, **delete** the following text from the second paragraph:

Deposits of material and growth of vegetation created them.

Make sure you delete the full stop as well.

2 Use the **Show/Hide** tool to check the spacing between the two remaining sentences of the second paragraph. There should be two spaces after the full stop.

3 Save the file keeping the filename **greatreef**.

Moving text

When text is moved in a document, it is removed from the original place and pasted in a new place.

▶▶ How to... *move text*

1 In your document, highlight the text to be moved. Make sure you also highlight any punctuation after the text.

2 In the **Formatting toolbar**, click on the **Cut** ✂ icon.

3 Click in the position that you want to paste the text.

4 Make sure you insert a space after a comma or two spaces after a full stop in the new position.

5 In the **Formatting toolbar**, click on the **Paste** 📋 icon.

6 The text is moved to the new place in the document.

1 In the file **greatreef**, **move** the following text in the third paragraph to become the **second** sentence of the **third** paragraph:

Many lagoon and ocean fish go to the reef to breed, feed on the reef plants or to catch prey.

Make sure you move the full stop as well.

2 Check the **spacing** by using the **Show/Hide** tool. There should be two spaces after a full stop.

3 Save the file keeping the filename **greatreef**.

Inserting text

You may want to add some additional words or sentences to an existing document. To do so, you will need to insert text.

Before you insert text

Before you enter any text, you will need to check that **OVR** (overwrite) in the **Status** bar is switched off (Figure 1.98). Look at the **Status bar** at the bottom of your Word screen. The OVR must be greyed out. If it is not greyed out, double-click on **OVR** to switch it off.

If the **OVR** is switched on, existing text will be deleted as you enter new text. If the **OVR** is turned off, you will simply be adding more text in between existing text.

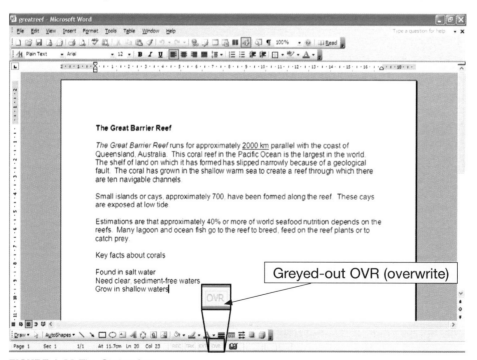

Greyed-out OVR (overwrite)

FIGURE 1.98 The Status bar

TIP!

The **OVR** button can be accidentally switched on if the **Insert (Ins)** key on the keyboard is pressed.

1 In your document, click with your mouse in the position where you want to insert text.

2 Make sure you insert a space after a comma or two spaces after a full stop in the new position.

3 Enter the required text.

4 Make sure you insert the correct spacing after the inserted text.

Check your understanding *Insert text*

1 In the file **greatreef**, go to the third sentence of the first paragraph ('The shelf of land …') and insert the text **below sea level** after 'has slipped narrowly' and before 'because of a'.

2 Check the spacing before and after the inserted text using the **Show/Hide** tool. There should be one space before and one space after the three inserted words.

3 Save the file keeping the filename **greatreef**.

4 Check your document **greatreef**. The positioning of text should appear as shown in Figure 1.99.

The Great Barrier Reef

The Great Barrier Reef runs for approximately 2000 km parallel with the coast of Queensland, Australia. This coral reef in the Pacific Ocean is the largest in the world. The shelf of land on which it has formed has slipped narrowly below sea level because of a geological fault. The coral has grown in the shallow warm sea to create a reef through which there are ten navigable channels.

Small islands or cays, approximately 700, have been formed along the reef. These cays are exposed at low tide.

Estimations are that approximately 40% or more of world seafood nutrition depends on the reefs. Many lagoon and ocean fish go to the reef to breed, feed on the reef plants or to catch prey.

Key facts about corals

Found in salt water
Need clear, sediment-free waters
Grow in shallow waters

FIGURE 1.99 The document **greatreef**

Find and Replace

You may want to change a word that appears more than once in your document. Using Find and Replace you can replace all instances of a particular word with a new word without having to look for it yourself. To ensure that all instances of the original word are replaced by the new word, you should let the computer carry out a **Find and Replace**.

1. In the **Menu bar**, click on **Edit**.

2. From the **Edit** menu, click on **Replace**.

3. The **Find and Replace** dialogue box is displayed.

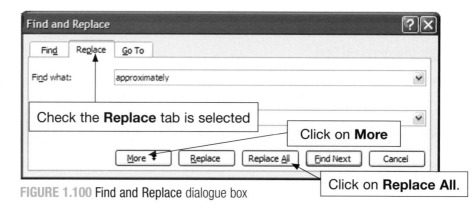

4. If the **Replace** tab is not selected, click on it (Figure 1.100).

Check the **Replace** tab is selected

Click on **More**

Click on **Replace All**.

FIGURE 1.100 Find and Replace dialogue box

5. In the **Find what** box, enter the word to be replaced.

6. In the **Replace with** box, enter the new word.

7. Click on **More**.

8. A **Search Options** menu is displayed.

9. To select **Find whole words only**, click in the box.

10. A tick appears in the box.

11. Click on **Replace All** to replace all instances of the original word with the new word.

TIP!

Do not click on **Replace** unless you want to replace only one occurrence of the word.

12. When Word has finished, a dialogue box displays telling you that Word has completed its search and the number of replacements that have been made (Figure 1.101).

13. Click on **OK**.

14. To close the **Find and Replace** dialogue box, click on **Close**.

FIGURE 1.101 A dialogue box confirming that Word has completed Find and Replace

Check your understanding *Use Find and Replace*

1. In the file **greatreef**, replace all instances of the word 'approximately' with the word **about** (three times in all).

2. Save your file, keeping the filename **greatreef**.

TIP!

It is good practice to tick the option box **Find whole words only** whether you are replacing a short or a long word.

Paragraph breaks and line spacing

A paragraph break is used to split a long paragraph to make it into two paragraphs.

BEFORE INSERTING A PARAGRAPH BREAK	AFTER INSERTING A PARAGRAPH BREAK
Accidents can be caused in offices by carelessness or thoughtlessness. It is the duty of everyone, from management to casual employees, to help prevent accidents in the workplace. An accident book should be kept to record details of all accidents and all treatments given, both to employees and to visitors to an organisation.	Accidents can be caused in offices by carelessness or thoughtlessness. It is the duty of everyone, from management to casual employees, to help prevent accidents in the workplace. An accident book should be kept to record details of all accidents and all treatments given, both to employees and to visitors to an organisation.

Text before and after inserting a paragraph break and a linespace

▶▶ How to... insert a paragraph break

1 In your document, click to place the cursor just before the first word of the sentence that will start the new paragraph.

2 Press the **Enter** key **twice**.

3 You should have one clear line space between two paragraphs.

4 Make sure the first word of the new paragraph starts at the left margin and does not have an unwanted space before it.

5 Click on the **Show/Hide** tool to check the spacing.

Check your understanding Insert paragraph break

1 In the file **greatreef**, insert a **paragraph break** in the first paragraph and a clear **line space** after the text ending '... largest in the world'.

2 Check the spacing before the paragraph break by using the **Show/Hide** tool:

   a There should be no dots representing spaces before the text 'The shelf of land...'.

   b There should be one paragraph marker between the two paragraphs and one paragraph marker after the text '... largest in the world'.

3 Save the file keeping the filename **greatreef**.

1 In your document, highlight the text to be changed.

2 In the **Menu bar**, click on **Format**.

3 From the **Format** menu, click on **Paragraph**.

4 A **Paragraph** dialogue box is displayed (Figure 1.102).

5 Check that the **Indents and Spacing** tab is selected.

6 In the **Spacing** section, click on the **down arrow** under **Line spacing**.

7 A drop-down menu is displayed.

8 Click on the line spacing option required, e.g. **Double**.

9 Click on **OK**.

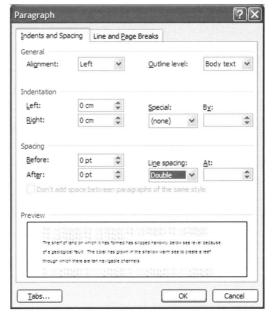

FIGURE 1.102 Paragraph dialogue box showing line spacing

10 The highlighted text is displayed in double line spacing.

11 Click outside the highlighted area to deselect the text.

Check your understanding *Change line spacing*

1 In the file **greatreef**, change the line spacing of the second paragraph to be **double line spacing**.

2 Use the **Show/Hide** tool to check that there is one paragraph marker above and below the paragraph.

3 Save the file keeping the filename **greatreef**.

Lists

Bulleted list

Below are examples of bulleted lists.

- *Found in salt water*
- *Need clear, sediment-free waters*
- *Grow in shallow waters*

➢ *Found in salt water*

➢ *Need clear, sediment-free waters*

➢ *Grow in shallow waters*

1 In your document, highlight the text to be bulleted.

2 Click on the **Bullets** ⫶☰ icon.

3 The selected text is displayed as a bulleted list. The style of the bullet character may be different on your computer.

4 Click elsewhere in your document to deselect the text.

Word may automatically indent bullets.

Numbered list

Below are examples of numbered lists.

1. Found in salt water
2. Need clear, sediment-free waters
3. Grow in shallow waters

1 Found in salt water
2 Need clear, sediment-free waters
3 Grow in shallow waters

1 In your document, highlight the text to be numbered.

2 Click on the **Numbering** ⫶☰ icon.

3 The selected text will display as a numbered list.

4 Click elsewhere in your document to deselect the text.

Word may automatically indent a numbered list.

Check your understanding **Create a bulleted list**

1 In the file **greatreef**, apply a bullet character to the following three lines of text:

Found in salt water

Need clear, sediment-free waters

Grow in shallow waters

2 Save the file keeping the filename **greatreef**.

Tabs and indents

Tabs are used to set the text further in from the left-hand margin.

Indented text looks like this.

Word has preset tab positions which appear as small grey lines just under the ruler. Tabs can also be created at specific measurements.

1 In your document, place the cursor before the text to be indented.

2 Make sure there are no spaces before the first letter of the text.

3 Press the Tab key.

4 The first line of text will be set further in from the left margin.

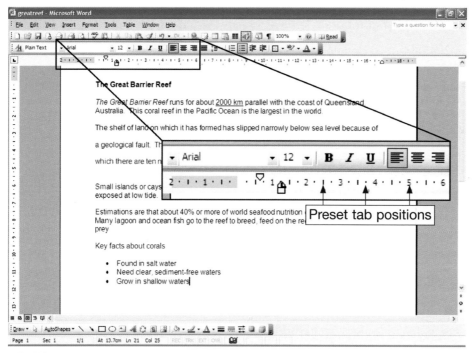

FIGURE 1.103 Ruler bar – arrows show tab positions that are already set

▶▶ How to... *create a new tab position*

1 In the **Menu bar**, click on **Format**.

2 From the **Format** menu, click on **Tabs**.

3 A **Tabs** dialogue box is displayed (Figure 1.104).

4 In the **Tab stop position** box, enter the new measurement.

5 Click on **Set**.

6 Click on **OK** to set the tab.

7 To indent the text, place the cursor before the text to be indented.

8 Press the **Tab** key.

9 The first line of text will be set in from the left margin to the tab position that you set.

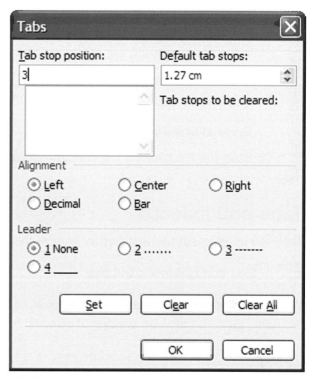

FIGURE 1.104 Tabs dialogue box

To set a tab, click on the required position on the ruler line. A tab will be set at that position (Figure 1.105).

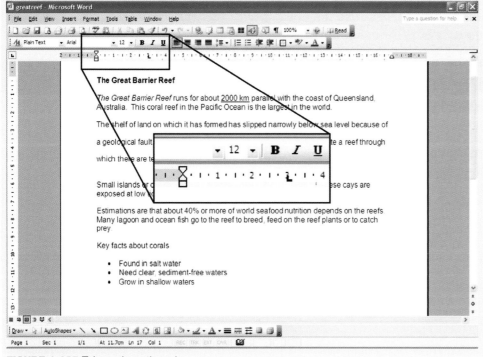

FIGURE 1.105 Tab mark on the ruler

1   In the file **greatreef**, set a tab at **3 cm** from the left-hand margin.

2   Indent the text **Key facts about corals** to the new tab position of **3 cm**.

3   Save your file, keeping the filename **greatreef**.

Tables

Tables can be used to display items in a document more clearly. Tables consist of columns and rows. Each box in the table is referred to as a cell. Tables can be displayed with or without outside borders and/or internal gridlines.

▶▶ How to... *insert a table*

1   In your document, place the cursor where the table is to be inserted.

2   In the **Menu bar**, click on **Table**.

3   From the **Table** menu, select **Insert** and then click on **Table**.

4 The **Insert Table** dialogue box is displayed (Figure 1.106).

5 Click in the **Number of columns** box and enter the number of columns. Alternatively, use the **up/down arrows** to do this.

6 Click in the **Number of rows** box and enter the number of rows or use the **up/down arrows**.

7 Click on **OK** to display the empty table in your document.

A table with 2 columns and 5 rows is shown below. Data is entered into the cells.

FIGURE 1.106 Insert Table dialogue box

Cell	Cell
Cell	Cell
Cell	Cell
Cell	Cell
Cell	Cell

TIP!

Click the button for **Fixed column width**. The width of each column will be the same.

▶▶ How to... *enter text in a table*

1 Place the cursor in the first cell (top left cell) of the table.

2 Enter the required text.

3 Press the **Tab** key or click in the next cell.

4 The cursor moves to the next column of the first row.

5 Enter the required text.

6 Press the **Tab** key again.

7 The cursor moves to the second row, first column.

8 Enter the rest of the text, pressing the Tab key to move from one cell to the next.

Displaying table borders and gridlines

Borders are the lines on the outside of the table (above, below, to the left and to the right). Gridlines are the divisions between the columns and the rows inside the table.

TIP!

Borders and gridlines may display automatically when you insert a table, but it is advisable to follow the steps on page 87 to make sure that dark borders will be clearly displayed on a printout.

display borders and gridlines on a table

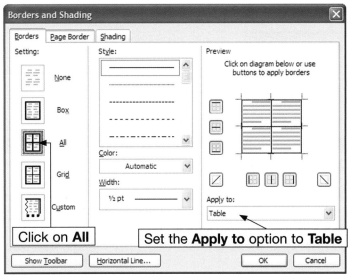

FIGURE 1.107 Borders and Shading dialogue box in the **Borders** tab view

1 To highlight the table, click in the top left cell of the table, hold down the **Shift** key, then click in the bottom right cell of the table.

2 In the **Menu bar**, click on **Format**.

3 From the **Format** menu, click on **Borders and Shading**.

4 The **Borders and Shading** dialogue box is displayed.

5 Select the **Borders** tab (Figure 1.107).

6 Under **Setting** click on **All**.

7 Under **Preview**, check that the **Apply to** option is set to **Table**.

8 Click on **OK** to display borders and gridlines on the table.

TIP!

To display borders, highlight a table, click on the **drop-down arrow** next to the **Outside Border** icon on the **Standard toolbar**, and click on the **All Borders** option (Figure 1.108).

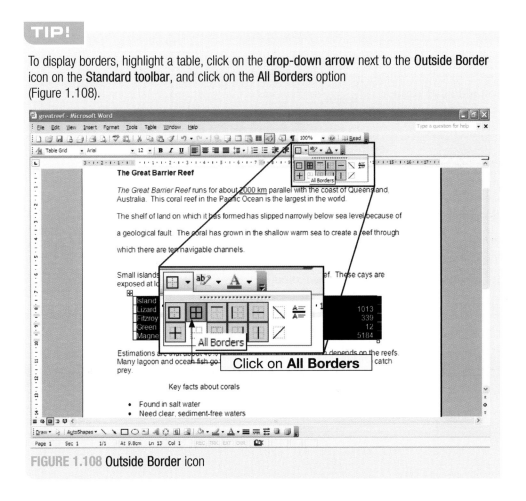

FIGURE 1.108 **Outside Border** icon

Applying shading to table cells

▶▶ How to... *apply shading to table cell(s)*

1 Highlight the table cells that are to be shaded by dragging your mouse over the required cells.

2 In the **Menu bar**, click on **Format**.

3 From the Format menu, click on **Borders and Shading**.

4 The **Borders and Shading** dialogue box is displayed.

5 Click on the **Shading** tab to select it (Figure 1.109).

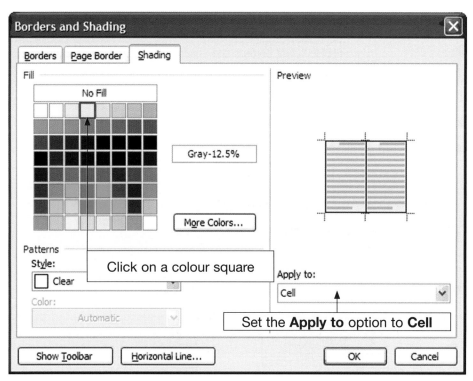

FIGURE 1.109 Borders and Shading dialogue box in the Shading tab view

6 Under **Fill**, click on a suitable colour square. Make sure you choose a colour that will allow any text in the cell to be read clearly.

7 Under **Preview**, check that the **Apply to** option is set to **Cell**.

8 Click on **OK** to apply shading to the highlighted cells.

9 Click in the document to deselect the cells.

1 In the file **greatreef**, insert a **paragraph break** and a clear **line space** at the end of the third paragraph after 'at low tide'.

2 Insert a **table** with **2 columns** and **5 rows**.

3 Enter the data below in the table:

Island	Size in hectares
Lizard Island	1013
Fitzroy Island	339
Green Island	12
Magnetic Island	5184

4 Make sure all table **borders** are displayed as shown above.

5 Format the text **Size in hectares** to be bold.

6 Right-align all the figures in the **Size in hectares** column.

7 Enter your name in the header or footer of the document.

8 Save the file keeping the filename **greatreef**.

Changing the column width of a table

When you insert a table in Word (and you choose the **Fixed Column Width** option), the table will extend from the left to the right margin. You may wish to reduce the width of the columns to improve the display. To do this you will need to have a good mouse and good mouse skills.

▶▶ How to... *change the column width of a table (optional)*

1 In the table, move the mouse pointer on to the left border of column one.

2 The mouse pointer turns into a double vertical line with arrows ◀‖▶.

3 Press and hold down the left mouse button, then drag the border to the right until the column width is reduced.

4 Release the left mouse button.

TIP!

Double-click on ◀‖▶. Word automatically adjusts the column width to fit the text within it.

Repeat this for column two as follows:

5 Move your mouse pointer on to the right border of column two.

6 The mouse pointer will turn into a double vertical line with arrows pointing both left and right.

7 Press and hold down the left mouse button, then drag the border to the left until the column width is reduced.

8 Release the left mouse button.

Word count

Word count is a feature that counts the number of words in a document or in selected text.

>> **How to...** *use word count*

1 In your document, highlight the selected text to be word counted OR, to count the number of words in the entire document, press **Ctrl** and **A** at the same time, which will highlight all the text in the document.

2 In the **Menu bar**, click on **Tools**.

3 From the **Tools** menu, click on **Word Count**.

4 The **Word Count** dialogue box is displayed (Figure 1.110).

5 The second item displays the number of words in the selected text. Make a note of this.

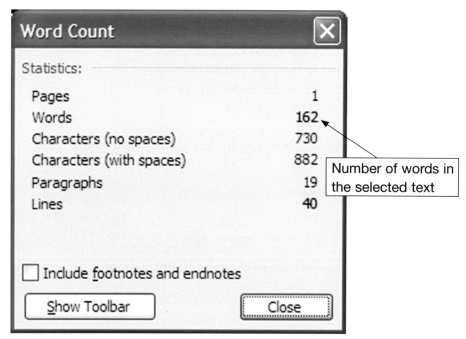

FIGURE 1.110 **Word Count** dialogue box

6 Click on **Close** to close the dialogue box

Check your understanding *Use word count*

1. In the file **greatreef**, carry out a **word count** to count the number of words in the whole document.
2. Enter the number of words at the end of the document. (You should have 162 words.)
3. Save the file, keeping the filename **greatreef**.
4. Print one copy of the file.
5. Close the file and exit **Word**.

Now, check your document **greatreef** against the screen print in Figure 1.111. Your table width and display of the word count may be different. The **Show/Hide** has been displayed to help you check your spacing.

The Great Barrier Reef

The Great Barrier Reef runs for about 2000 km parallel with the coast of Queensland, Australia. This coral reef in the Pacific Ocean is the largest in the world.

The shelf of land on which it has formed has slipped narrowly below sea level because of a geological fault. The coral has grown in the shallow warm sea to create a reef through which there are ten navigable channels.

Small islands or cays, about 700, have been formed along the reef. These cays are exposed at low tide.

Island	**Size in hectares**
Lizard Island	1013
Fitzroy Island	339
Green Island	12
Magnetic Island	5184

Estimations are that about 40% or more of world seafood nutrition depends on the reefs. Many lagoon and ocean fish go to the reef to breed, feed on the reef plants or to catch prey.

Key facts about corals

- Found in salt water
- Need clear, sediment-free waters
- Grow in shallow waters

162 words

FIGURE 1.111 The final document **greatreef**, with **Show/Hide** tool switched on

By working through Section 2 you will have learnt the skills below. Read each item to help you decide how confident you feel about each skill.

- ○ open an existing file and save it using a different filename
- ○ use bold, italic and underline
- ○ delete text
- ○ move text
- ○ insert text
- ○ use **Find and Replace**
- ○ insert paragraph break
- ○ change line spacing
- ○ use bullets and numbering
- ○ use tabs and indents
- ○ insert a table
- ○ display borders and gridlines for a table
- ○ apply shading to table cell(s)
- ○ apply alignment to text in a table
- ○ use word count
- ○ save an updated document
- ○ print an updated document.

If you think you need more practice on any of the skills above, go back and work through the skill(s) again.

If you feel confident, do the Build-up and Practice tasks.

Click means click with the left mouse button

QUICK REFERENCE – File management

HOW TO...	METHOD	QUICK METHOD	USING MENUS
All file management tasks must be done in your user area through the My Computer window			
Create a folder	In the File and Folder Tasks box → Click on Make a new folder → New Folder is displayed → Press Backspace to delete the words New Folder → Type the required folder name → Press Enter	In your user area → Right-click → New → Folder → 'New Folder' → Press Backspace to delete the words New Folder → Enter new name → Enter	File menu → New → Folder → Delete 'New Folder' → Enter new name → Enter
Create a subfolder	Double-click to open folder → In the File and Folder Tasks box → Click on Make a new folder → New Folder is displayed → Press Backspace to delete the words 'New Folder' → Enter the required subfolder name → Press Enter	Open relevant folder → Right click → New → Folder → 'New Folder' → Enter new name → Enter	Double-click to open existing folder → File menu → New → Folder → Delete 'New Folder' → Enter new name → Enter
Rename a file	Click on the file you want to rename → In the File and Folder Tasks box → Click on Rename this file → Press Backspace to delete the existing name → Enter the new filename → Press Enter	Right-click on existing file → Click on Rename → Delete existing name → Enter new name → Enter	Click on file → File menu → Rename → Delete existing name → Enter new name → Enter
Rename a folder	Click on the folder you want to rename → In the File and Folder Tasks box → Click on Rename this folder → Press Backspace to delete the existing name → Enter the new folder name → Press Enter	Right-click on existing folder → Click on Rename → Delete existing name → Enter new name → Enter	Click on folder → File menu → Rename → Delete existing name → Enter new name → Enter
Delete a file	Click on the file you want to delete → In the File and Folder Tasks box → Click on Delete this file → A Confirm File Delete dialogue box displays → Click on Yes	Click on file → Right-click → Delete OR click on file → press Delete key → a Confirm File Delete dialogue box displays → Click on Yes	Click on file → File menu → Delete → a Confirm File Delete dialogue box displays → Click on Yes

HOW TO...	METHOD	QUICK METHOD	USING MENUS
	All file management tasks must be done in your user area through the My Computer window		
Delete a folder	Click on the folder you want to delete → In the File and Folder Tasks box → Click on Delete this folder → A Confirm Folder Delete dialogue box displays → Click on Yes	Click on folder → Right-click → Delete OR click on folder → Press Delete key	Click on folder → File menu → Delete → a Confirm Folder Delete dialogue box displays → Click on Yes
Move a file	Click on the file you want to move → In the File and Folder Tasks box → Click on Move this file → A Move Items dialogue box displays → Select the folder that you want to move the file into → Click on Move	Right-click on file → Cut → Go to folder that you want to move file to → Right-click → Paste	Click on file → Edit menu → Cut → Go to folder that you want to move file to → Double-click to open folder → Edit menu → Paste
Move a folder	Click on the folder you want to move → In the File and Folder Tasks box → Click on Move this folder → A Move Items dialogue box displays → Select the folder that you want to move the folder into → Click on Move	Right-click on folder → Cut → Go to folder that you want to move folder to → Right-click → Paste	Click on folder → Edit menu → Cut → Go to folder that you want to move folder to → Double-click to open folder → Edit menu → Paste
Copy a file	Click on the file you want to copy → In the File and Folder Tasks box → Click on Copy this file → A Copy Items dialogue box displays → Click on the folder name in your user area that you want to copy the file to → Click on Copy	Right-click on file → Copy → Use the Back button in the toolbar to go to the folder that you want to copy file to → Right-click → Paste	Click on file → Edit menu → Copy → Go to folder that you want to copy file to → Double-click to open folder → Edit menu → Paste
Copy a folder	Click on the folder you want to copy → In the File and Folder Tasks box → Click on Copy this folder → A Copy Items dialogue box displays → Click on the folder name in your user area that you want to copy the folder to → Click on Copy	Right-click on folder → Copy → Use the Back button in the toolbar to go to the folder that you want to copy folder to → Right-click → Paste	Click on folder → Edit menu → Copy → Go to folder that you want to copy folder to → Double-click to open folder → Edit menu → Paste

HOW TO...	METHOD	QUICK METHOD	USING MENUS
All file management tasks must be done in your user area through the My Computer window			
Take a screen print of folder structure	Double-click to open the folder for which you want to take a screen print of the contents → Press Alt and Print Screen at the same time → Load Microsoft Word → Start → Programs → Microsoft Office → Microsoft Office Word 2003 → In blank document → Click on the Paste icon	Go to user area → Open folder that you want to screen print → Alt + Print Screen keys at the same time (or Print Screen key only) → Open Word document → Right-click in document → Menu displays → Paste	Go to user area → Open folder that you want to screen print → Alt + Print Screen keys at the same time (or Print Screen key only) → Open Word document → Edit menu → Paste
Save the screen print (Tip! Paste all your screen prints into one Word document)	In Word click on the File menu → Click on Save → Save As dialogue box displays → Click on the down arrow to the right of the Save in box, then click on your user area → In the filename row → Delete any text → Enter the required filename → Click on Save	Click on the Save icon → Save As dialogue box displays → Make sure you save into the correct folder → Enter a filename → Save OR press Ctrl + S to open Save As window	File menu → Save As → Make sure you save into the correct folder → Delete existing text, enter a filename → Save
Print your screen print	Click on the Print icon	Click on the Print icon	File menu → Print → OK
Close a document and exit Word	Click on the Close (red cross) icon at the top right of the window	Click on the Close (red cross) icon at the top right of the window	File menu → Close → File menu → Exit
Close the My Computer window	Click on the Close (red cross) icon at the top right	Click on the Close (red cross) icon at the top right	File menu → Close

Click means click with the left mouse button

QUICK REFERENCE – Create a new document

Keep a copy of this page next to you. Refer to it when working through tasks and during any assessments.

HOW TO...	METHOD	QUICK METHOD	USING MENUS
Start Word	Click on Start → All Programs → Microsoft Office → Microsoft Office Word 2003	Click on the Word icon on the Quick Launch bar OR double-click on the Word icon on the desktop	Start → All Programs → Microsoft Office → Microsoft Office Word 2003
Create a new document	Click on File menu → New (Note: a new blank document opens when you load Word)	Click on the New icon on the toolbar	File menu → New
Set orientation	Click on File menu → Page Setup → Margins tab → Click on Portrait or Landscape → Click on OK	Double-click on the blue part of Ruler bar → Page Setup dialogue box opens → Click on Portrait or Landscape → OK	File → Page Setup → Margins tab → Click on Portrait or Landscape → OK
Set margins	Click on File menu → Page Setup → Margins tab → Enter the measurement for each margin or use the up/down arrows → Click on OK	Double-click on the blue part of Ruler bar → Page Setup dialogue box displays → Enter required margins OR use up/down arrows → OK	File → Page Setup → Margins tab → Enter required margins or use up/down arrows → OK
Set line spacing	Click on Format menu → Paragraph → Indents and Spacing tab → Line spacing → Click on drop-down arrow → Select an option → Click on OK	Single line spacing is set as default. To set double line spacing, press the Ctrl and 2 keys together	Highlight text → Format menu → Paragraph → Click on down arrow next to Line spacing box → Select option → OK
Set font size before entering text	Click on drop-down arrow next to Font Size on toolbar → Click on required size	Click on the drop-down arrow next to Font Size on toolbar → Click on required size	Format menu → Font → Size → OK

HOW TO...	METHOD	QUICK METHOD	USING MENUS
Set font size after entering text	Highlight relevant text → Click on drop-down arrow next to Font Size on toolbar → Click on required size	Highlight text → Click on Ctrl and [to decrease text size by one point at a time. Click Ctrl and] to increase text size by one point at a time. [ ] are square brackets on the keyboard	Highlight text → Format menu → Font → Size → OK
Set font type before entering text	Click on drop-down arrow next to Font on toolbar → Click on required font name	Click on drop-down arrow next to Font on toolbar → Click on required font name	Format menu → Font → Font name → OK
Set font type after entering text	Highlight relevant text → Click on drop-down arrow next to Font on toolbar → Click on font name	Highlight relevant text → Click on drop-down arrow next to Font on toolbar → Click on font name	Highlight text → Format menu → Font → Font name → OK
Align text before entering text	Click on the Align Left, Align Right, Center align or Justify icon on toolbar	Left align: Ctrl + L Right align: Ctrl + R Fully justify: Ctrl + J Centre: Ctrl + E	Format menu → Paragraph → Click on drop-down arrow next to Alignment → Click on required alignment → OK
Align text after entering text	Highlight relevant text → Click on the Align Left, Align Right, Center align or Justify icon	Highlight relevant text → Left align: Ctrl + L Right align: Ctrl + R Fully justify: Ctrl + J Centre: Ctrl + E	Highlight relevant text → Format menu → Paragraph → Click on drop-down arrow next to Alignment → Click on required alignment → OK

HOW TO...	METHOD	QUICK METHOD	USING MENUS
Set or check the language	Click on Tools menu → Language → Set Language → Set language to English (U.K.) → Click on OK	Language (English U.K.) may be displayed on Status bar (depends on your computer settings)	Tools menu → Language → Set Language → Set language to English (U.K.) → OK
Spell check	Click on Spelling and Grammar icon → If Word finds an error → Spelling and Grammar dialogue box displays → Incorrect word is highlighted in red in Not in dictionary box → Alternatives may be given in Suggestions box → Click on correct suggestion → Click on Change	Click on the Spelling and Grammar icon → Spelling and Grammar dialogue box displays → Incorrect word is highlighted in red in Not in dictionary box → Alternatives may be given in Suggestions box → Click on correct suggestion → Change	Tools menu → Spelling and Grammar → Spelling and Grammar dialogue box displays → Incorrect word is highlighted in red in Not in dictionary box → Alternatives may be given in Suggestions box → Click on correct suggestion → Change
Check spelling as you type	Right-click within word underlined in red → List of suggestions displays → Click on correct option from suggested list	Default is to check spelling as you type → Incorrect words underlined in red → Right-click within Word → Choose correct suggestion	Tools menu → Options → Spelling and Grammar tab → Make sure there is a tick in Check spelling as you type box → Incorrectly spelt words will be underlined in red
Use Show/Hide tool to check document	Click on Show/Hide icon on toolbar → Check for one dot between words, one dot after comma, two dots after full stop, one paragraph marker at the end of a paragraph and one paragraph marker between paragraphs	Click on Show/Hide icon on toolbar → Check for one dot between words, one dot after comma, two dots after full stop, one paragraph marker at the end of a paragraph and one paragraph marker between paragraphs	Click on Show/Hide icon on toolbar → Check for one dot between words, one dot after comma; two dots after full stop, one paragraph marker at the end of a paragraph and one paragraph marker between paragraphs

HOW TO...	METHOD	QUICK METHOD	USING MENUS
Save a Word document	Click on File menu → Click on Save As → Save As dialogue box displays → Click on down arrow to right of Save in box, then click on your user area → In File name box, delete any existing text → Enter required filename → Click on Save	Click on the Save icon → In Save As dialogue box → Click on down arrow to the right of the Save in box, then click on your user area → In File name box, delete any existing text → Enter required filename → Click on Save OR press Ctrl + S to open Save As dialogue box	File menu → Save As → In Save As dialogue box → Click on down arrow to the right of the Save in box, then click on your user area → In File name box, delete any existing text → Enter required filename → Save
Save a Word document into a new folder from within Word	Click on File menu → Click on Save As → Save As dialogue box displays → Click on down arrow to right of Save in box, then click on your user area → Click on the Create New Folder icon → New Folder dialogue box opens → Enter new folder name → Click on OK → In File name box delete any existing text → Enter required filename → Click on Save	Click on the Save icon → Enter a filename → Click on Create New Folder → Enter new folder name → OK → Make sure you save into the correct folder/user area → Save	File menu → Save As → Enter a filename → Click on Create New Folder → Enter new folder name → Make sure you save into the correct folder/user area → Save
Save an existing document	Click on File menu → Click on Save	Click on the Save icon OR press Ctrl + S	File menu → Save
Print a document	Click on File menu → Click on Print → Print dialogue box displays → Check Page Range is set to All → Set Number of copies to 1 → Click on OK	Click on the Print icon	File menu → Print → OK

HOW TO...	METHOD	QUICK METHOD	USING MENUS
Add a header or footer	Click on View menu → Click on Header and Footer → Enter required information in header → Click on Switch between Header and Footer icon → Enter required information in footer → Click on Close	Click on View menu → Click on Header and Footer → Enter the required information in the header → Click on the Switch Between Header and Footer icon → Enter any required information in the footer → Don't click Close until you've added all headers and footers. In Print Layout view, if there are headers/footers entered → Double-click on header/footer to open header/footer window quickly	View menu → Header and Footer → Enter required information in the header → Click on Switch Between Header and Footer icon → Enter required information in footer → Close
Add an automatic date	Click on View menu → Click on Header and Footer → Click on Insert Date icon → Click on Close		View menu → Header and Footer → Click on Insert Date icon → Close
Add an automatic filename	Click on View menu → Click on Header and Footer → Click on the drop-down arrow next to Insert AutoText → Click on Filename → Click on Close → Use Print Preview to check		View menu → Header and Footer → Click on the drop-down arrow next to Insert AutoText → Click on Filename → Close
Close a document	Click on File menu → Click on Close	Click on the black cross to close the document	File menu → Close
Exit Word	Click on File menu → Click on Exit	Click on the red cross to exit Word	File menu → Exit
Close a document and exit Word	Click on File menu → Click on Close → Click on File menu→ Click on Exit	Click on the red cross to close any open documents and exit Word	File menu → Close → File menu → Exit

Click means click with the left mouse button

Keep a copy of this page next to you. Refer to it when working through tasks and during any assessments.

QUICK REFERENCE – *Edit a document*

HOW TO...	METHOD	QUICK METHOD	USING MENUS
Save an existing document with a new filename	Click on File menu ⤳ Save As ⤳ Save As dialogue box displays ⤳ Click on down arrow to right of Save in ⤳ Click on user area ⤳ In Filename box ⤳ Delete existing filename ⤳ Enter new filename ⤳ Click on down arrow to the right of Save as type box ⤳ Click on Word Document ⤳ Click on Save	Press Alt + F keys ⤳ File menu displays ⤳ Press A key ⤳ Save As dialogue box displays ⤳ Click on down arrow next to Save in box ⤳ Click on user area ⤳ In File name box ⤳ Delete existing filename ⤳ Enter new filename ⤳ Click on down arrow to the right of Save as type box ⤳ Click on Word Document ⤳ Save	File menu ⤳ Save As ⤳ Save As dialogue box displays ⤳ Click on down arrow to right of Save in box ⤳ Click on user area ⤳ In File name box ⤳ Delete existing filename ⤳ Enter new filename ⤳ Click on down arrow to the right of Save as type box ⤳ Click on Word Document ⤳ Save
Format text to be bold	Highlight text ⤳ Click on Bold icon ⤳ Click elsewhere in document to deselect text	Highlight text ⤳ Ctrl + B OR click on the Bold icon	Highlight text ⤳ Format menu ⤳ Font ⤳ Bold ⤳ OK
Format text to be italic	Highlight text ⤳ Click on the Italic icon ⤳ Click elsewhere in document to deselect text	Highlight text ⤳ Ctrl + I OR click on the Italic icon	Highlight text ⤳ Format menu ⤳ Font ⤳ Italic ⤳ OK
Underline text	Highlight text ⤳ Click on the Underline icon ⤳ Click elsewhere in document to deselect text	Highlight text ⤳ Ctrl + U OR click on the Underline icon	Highlight text ⤳ Format menu ⤳ Font ⤳ Click on drop-down arrow below Underline style ⤳ OK
Delete text	Highlight relevant text including any associated punctuation ⤳ Click on the Cut icon	Highlight text ⤳ Press Delete key	Highlight text ⤳ Edit menu ⤳ Cut

HOW TO...	METHOD	QUICK METHOD	USING MENUS
Move text	Highlight relevant text including any associated punctuation → Click on the Cut icon → Click in new position → Insert correct spacing → Click on the Paste icon	Highlight text → Click and drag highlighted text to new position	Highlight text → Edit menu → Cut → Place cursor in new position → Edit menu → Paste
Insert text	Check that OVR is switched off (greyed out) in Status bar → Click in position that you want to insert text → Insert correct spacing → Enter text → Insert correct spacing after inserted text	Place cursor in required place → Enter text	N/A
Find and replace	Click on Edit menu → Click on Replace → Find and Replace dialogue box displays → In Find what box, enter word to replace → In Replace with box, enter new word → Click on More → Tick Find whole words only → Click on Replace All → Click on OK → Click on Close	Press Ctrl + H keys → In Find what box, enter word to replace → In Replace with box, enter new word → Click on More → Tick Find whole words only → Replace All → OK → Close	Edit menu → Replace → Find and Replace dialogue box displays → In Find what box, enter word to be replaced → In Replace with box, enter new word → More → Tick Find whole words only → Replace All → OK → Close
Insert a paragraph break	Place cursor just before the first word of the sentence that will start the new paragraph → Press Enter key twice → Click on the Show/Hide tool icon to check spacing is correct	Place cursor in required position → Press Enter key on the keyboard twice	N/A
Change line spacing	Highlight relevant text → Click on Format menu → Click on Paragraph → Paragraph dialogue box displays → Indents and Spacing tab → Click on down arrow below Line spacing → Click on line spacing option required → Click on OK → Click outside the highlighted area to deselect text	Highlight text → Double line spacing: Ctrl + 2 Single line spacing: Ctrl + 1	Highlight text → Format menu → Paragraph → Paragraph dialogue box displays → Indents and Spacing tab → Click on the down arrow under Line spacing → Click on line spacing required → OK → Click outside the highlighted area to remove the highlight

HOW TO...	METHOD	QUICK METHOD	USING MENUS
Create a bulleted list	Highlight relevant text → Click on Bullets icon	Highlight text → Click on the Bullets icon	Highlight text → Format menu → Bullets and Numbering → Click on required bullet style → OK
Create a numbered list	Highlight relevant text → Click on Numbering icon	Highlight text → Click on Numbering icon	Highlight text → Format menu → Bullets and Numbering → Click on Numbered tab → Click on required number style → OK
Indent text to a preset tab position	Place the cursor before the text → Make sure there are no spaces before the first letter of the text → Press the Tab key	Place cursor in front of text → Press Tab key	N/A
Create a new tab position and indent text	Click on Format menu → Click on Tabs → In the Tab stop position enter new measurement → Click on Set → Click on OK → \n\nTo indent the text, place the cursor before the text → Press Tab key	Click on required position on Ruler bar → Place cursor in front of text → Press Tab key	Format menu → Tabs → Enter measurement → Set → OK → \n\nTo indent text, place the cursor before the text → Press Tab key
Insert a table	Place cursor in correct position → Click on the Table menu → Click on Insert → Click on Table → Insert Table dialogue box displays → Click in Number of columns box and enter number of columns required → Click in Number of rows box and enter number of rows required → Click on OK	Click on the Insert Table icon → Drag your mouse over the required number of rows and columns (option is limited to 5 columns and 4 rows) → Release mouse button	Table menu → Insert → Table → Insert Table dialogue box displays → Click in the Number of columns box and enter the number of columns → Click in the Number of rows box and enter the number of rows → OK

HOW TO...	METHOD	QUICK METHOD	USING MENUS
Enter text in table	Place cursor in first cell of the table → Enter text → press Tab key to move from cell to cell (or click in relevant cell)	Place cursor in first table cell → Enter text → Press Tab key to move from cell to cell	N/A
Display table borders and gridlines	Highlight table as follows → Click in top left cell of table, hold down the Shift key then click in bottom right cell of table → Click on Format menu → Click on Borders and Shading → In Borders tab → Click on All → Check Apply to is set to Table → Click on OK	Highlight table → Click in top left cell, hold down Shift key, then click in bottom right cell → Click on drop-down arrow next to Borders icon on toolbar → Select All Borders option	Click in Table → Table menu → Table Properties → Borders and Shading → Borders tab → All → OK
Change the column width of a table	Move your mouse on column border → Pointer turns into a double arrow → Drag border to change column width	Move mouse pointer on border → Double arrows display on border → Drag border to change column width	Click in Table → Table menu → Table Properties → Column tab → Use up/down arrows to change measurement or enter required measurement → OK
Use word count	Highlight relevant text → Click on Tools menu → Click on Word Count → Word Count dialogue box displays → Number of words is second item → Click on Close → Click in the document to deselect the text	Highlight relevant text → Click on Tools menu → Click on Word Count → Word Count dialogue box displays → Number of words is second item → Close → Click in the document to deselect the text	Highlight relevant text → Tools menu → Word Count → Word Count dialogue box displays → Second item number displays the number of words → Close → Click in the document to deselect the text

PRACTICE TASK ❶ *Use a computer*

Answer the following questions:

1 What is the term for all the physical parts of a computer, e.g. monitor, keyboard, that you can see and touch?

2 How do you display the **Start** menu?

3 Why is it important to take a break from looking at the computer screen?

4 Which two keys should be used to enter the J of John?

5 Which mouse button would you press to right-click?

6 Which two keys would you press to take a screen print?

7 What is the term used to describe the action when the left mouse button is pressed quickly twice?

8 What term is used to describe the programs that allow you to use the computer?

9 What does RSI stand for?

10 You might have to use a password when logging on to a computer. When else might you need to use a password?

11 What is the term used to describe small pictures on the desktop screen?

12 What is the name of the bar that usually runs along the bottom of the computer screen?

13 Which option would you select from the **Start** menu to close down the computer?

For this task, you will need the following folders and files from the **files_chapter1** folder:

○ the folder **task1** containing three text files: **autumn, spring, summer** (Figure 1.55)

○ the subfolder **t1files** containing:

– an image file: **daffy**

– a text file: **winter** (Figure 1.56).

FIGURE 1.55 The folder task1

1a Rename the folder **task1** to be your **name (first and last name)**.

b In this folder create a new subfolder **seasons**.

2 Copy the text file **spring** to the subfolder **seasons**.

3 Move the text file **summer** from the folder **your name** into the subfolder **seasons**.

4 Delete the folder **t1files** and its contents.

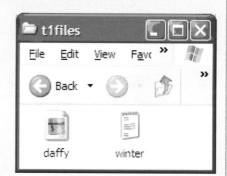

FIGURE 1.56 The subfolder t1files

5 Take a screen print as evidence of the folder **your name (first and last name)** and the contents of this folder.

6 Take a screen print of the subfolder **seasons** and the contents of this folder.

7 Enter your **name** and today's **date** in the document containing the screen prints.

8 Save the screen print(s) into your user area using suitable filename(s). (On your screen print, you are not expected to show the saved file(s) containing the screen print.)

9 The file(s) containing your screen prints may be saved in any folder in your user area.

10 Print the file(s) containing the screen prints. Make sure that all the contents of the folders and the subfolder are clearly visible on the printout.

11 Close any open files.

BUILD-UP TASK ② Create a new document

1 Create a new word processing document.

2 Set the page orientation to **portrait**.

3 Set the **top**, **left** and **right** page margins to **3.3 cm**.

4 Set the font type to **Arial**.

5 Set the font size to **12**.

6 a Enter the following text in **single line spacing**.

b Make sure the text is **fully justified**.

THE VICTORIA FALLS

The Zambezi River trickles to life in the highlands of north-west Zambia and meanders through the plains. Then the route becomes more hazardous, with rocky gorges, some narrow, others over a kilometre long.

The River passes through palm-fringed banks before it becomes turbulent, gathering strength for its mighty leap over the cliffs to form what is now known to the world as the Victoria Falls.

Five separate falls make up the Victoria Falls: Devil's Cataract, Main Falls, Horseshoe Falls, Rainbow Falls and Eastern Cataract. In flood season, 545 million litres of water a minute crash down the 100-metre height of the Falls along their 1688-metre width.

7 Save the file using the filename **wptask1** in a new folder called **wordpro**.

BUILD-UP TASK ③ Create a new document

1 Continue working in your saved file **wptask1**.

2 a In the header, enter your **name** and **centre number**.

b In the footer, insert an **automatic date** and an **automatic filename**.

c The headers and footers may be in any font size and style.

3 a Check the file for any errors and carry out a spell check.

b Save the file keeping the filename **wptask1** in the folder **wordpro**.

c Use **Print Preview** to check the automatic filename **wptask1** in the footer.

d Print the file **wptask1**.

4 Close the file **wptask1**.

5 Exit Word.

Before you begin this task, check that you have a copy of the folder **files_chapter2** in your user area. The file called **france**, which you will need for this task, is in the folder.

1 Open the file called **france**.

2 Save the file **france** using the filename **tourism**.

3 In the first paragraph, insert a **paragraph break** and a clear **line space** after the second sentence ending '. . . Mont Saint Michel'.

4 a At the end of the third paragraph, insert a **paragraph break** and a clear **line space**.

 b Create a table with **2 columns** and **5 rows**.

 c Enter the data below in the table:

Tours	Cost in Euros
Visit with commentary	4.50
Visit with audio guide	5.00
Unaccompanied visit	5.50
Guided visit	5.50

 d Make sure all borders will be displayed for the table on the printout, as shown above.

 e Make sure there is one clear **line space** after the table.

 f Format the table heading **Tours** to be **bold**.

 g **Centre** the heading **Cost in Euros**.

 h The remaining text and numbers should be **left-aligned**.

5 Enter your **name** in the header.

6 Insert an **automatic date** and an **automatic filename** in the footer.

7 Save your file keeping the filename **tourism**.

8 Close the file.

You will make some amendments to the file **tourism** that you saved in Build-up task 4 Edit a document.

1 Open the file **tourism**.

2 In the first paragraph, insert the following text as the last sentence: **This inspired the bishop to build the original abbey**.

3 In the first paragraph, delete the text: **and the Disney Resort**
  Do not delete the comma after Resort.

4 In the third paragraph, move the text: **Three million tourists go to Mont Saint Michel every year.** to be the last sentence of the third paragraph.

5 a Apply a **bullet** character to the following three lines of text:

   Paris
   Disney Resort
   Mont Saint Michel

  b Apply **double line spacing** to the bulleted text only.

  c Indent the text **Popular destinations** so that it is set in from the left margin.

6 Replace the word **visitors** with the word **tourists** wherever it occurs (three times in all).

7 Check the text for accuracy.

8 Save the file keeping the filename **tourism**.

9 a Using the software facility, carry out a **word count** in the file.

  b Enter the number of words on your printout at least two lines below the bulleted list. You may use any alignment for this.

10 Save the file keeping the filename **tourism**.

11 Print the file **tourism**.

12 Close the file.

PRACTICE TASK

Task 1

For this task, you will need the following folders and files from the **files_chapter1** folder:

○ the folder **task2** containing:

– two text files: **jul** and **sep**

– an image file: **jun** (Figure 1.57)

○ the subfolder **t2files** containing:

– an image file: **may**

– a text file: **nov** (Figure 1.58).

1 a Rename the folder **task2** to: **years**.

b In this folder create a new subfolder: **months**.

2 Copy the image file **jun** to the subfolder **months**.

3 Move the text file **jul** from the folder **years** into the subfolder **months**.

4 Delete the file **sep** from the folder **years**.

a Take a screen print as evidence of the folder **years** and its contents.

b Take a screen print of the subfolder **months** and its contents.

c Enter your **name** and today's **date** in this document.

d Save the screen print(s) into your user area using suitable filename(s). (On your screen print, you are not expected to show the saved file(s) containing the screen print.)

e The file(s) containing your screen prints may be saved in any folder in your user area.

f Print the file(s) containing the screen prints. Make sure that all the contents of the folders and the subfolders are clearly visible on the printout.

5 Close any open files.

FIGURE 1.57 The folder **task2**

FIGURE 1.58 The subfolder **t2files**

Task 2

1 Create a new word processing document.

2 Set the page orientation to **landscape**.

3 Set the **top, left** and **right** page margins to **2.5 cm**.

4 Set the font type to **Times New Roman**.

5 Set the font size to **14**.

6 a Enter the following text in **double line spacing**.

b Make sure the text is **left-aligned**.

TIP!

When you enter **th** after 19, Word will automatically make it superscript

The World on a Plate

Volcanoes and earthquakes are more common in some parts of the world than others. Although this was known in the early 19th century, it was not until the 1960s, when the secrets of the deep ocean floor began to be revealed, that scientists found an explanation.

This became known as the theory of plate tectonics. "Tectonic" is a Greek word that means building. These tectonic plates move across the Earth's surface in response to forces and movements deep within the planet. The plate boundaries, where plates collide, rub or move, are areas of intense geological activity.

Volcanoes and earthquakes occur at these boundaries (the nature of the boundary dictates the nature of the eruption that occurs there).

7 a **Centre** the heading.

b Format the heading to be **bold** and **italic**.

8 a In the header, insert an **automatic date** and an **automatic filename**.

b In the footer, enter your **name** and **centre number**.

9 a Check the file for any errors and carry out a spell check.

b Save the file with the filename **wptask2** in the folder **wordpro** that you created earlier. Use **Print Preview** to check the automatic filename **wptask2** in the footer.

10 Print the file **wptask2**.

11 Close the file **wptask2**.

12 Exit Word.

Task 3

Before you begin this task, check that you have a copy of the folder **files_chapter2** in your user area. The file called **america**, which you will need for this task, is in the folder.

1 Open the file **america.**

2 Save the file **america** using the filename **chicago**.

3 a Set a new tab at **1.5 cm**.

   b Tab the text **Chicago is recognised for its** so that this text is indented **1.5 cm** from the left margin.

4 Apply a **bullet** character to the following six lines of text:

   music and theatrical achievements
   sporting greats
   shops
   range of restaurants
   museums
   art displays.

5 In the paragraph beginning **Lake Michigan is the…** insert a **paragraph break** and a clear **line space** after the second sentence ending… **United States and Canada**.

6 Create a **table** with **2 columns** and **4 rows** below the final paragraph, leaving one clear **line space** after the paragraph.

   a Enter the data below in the table:

Attraction	Annual Visitors
Navy Pier	5325000
Adler Planetarium	458357
Sears Tower Skydeck	1363824

   b Make sure all borders will be displayed for the table on the printout, as shown above.

   c Make sure all data in the table is fully displayed.

7 **Centre** the table headings only.

8 Format the table headings to be **italic**.

9 Save the file keeping the filename **chicago**.

Task 4

Edit the file **chicago** as follows:

1 In the first paragraph, insert a paragraph break and a clear line space after the text… **the "Second City"**.

2 In the final paragraph, insert the text **pedestrians and cyclists** after the text… **with many joggers,**

3 In the paragraph beginning **Typical things**… move the text **Wrigley Field baseball,** to be after the text **…with Chicago are**…

4 Delete only the text **…and theatrical achievements** from the first bullet.

5 Apply **double line spacing** to the first paragraph only beginning **Chicago is a…**

6 Replace the word **range** with the word **variety** wherever it occurs (three times in all).

7 Using the software facility, carry out a word count in the file.

8 Enter the number of words on your printout at least two lines below the table. You may use any alignment for this.

9 Insert your **name** and **centre number** in the header.

10 Insert an **automatic date** and an **automatic filename** in the footer.

11 Check your text for accuracy.

12 Save your file, keeping the filename **chicago**.

13 Print the file **chicago**.

14 Close the file and exit Word.

The solutions for the Build-up and Practice tasks can be found in the folder **worked_copies_unit1** on the CD-ROM.

Definition of terms

Alignment	How the text lines up with the left and right margins. Text can be aligned to the left, centre, right or text can be fully justified.
Application software	Application software allows you to carry out specific tasks. There are many different types of software programs.
Backspace key	A key that deletes characters to the left of the cursor.
Boot up	A process by which the computer prepares itself for use. Also referred to as **load up**.
Caps Lock	A key on the keyboard which, when switched on, allows all text to be entered in upper case.
CPU	The central processing unit – the 'brain' of the computer.
Data	Information (e.g. text, numbers, images) that is processed and produced by a computer.
Default	The setting or value that a computer program (or system) is given as a standard setting. It is likely to be the setting that 'most people' would choose.
Delete	To delete currently selected data, e.g. text.
Desktop	The display on the monitor when the computer is first switched on.
Dialogue box	Also spelled dialog box. A window that displays options.
Document	A file.
Drive	A device that stores information. It can be external (zip drive) or fixed into the computer (e.g. C: drive).
Edit	To make changes to a document e.g. cut, copy, delete, insert, Find and Replace.
Emphasis	Emphasis is used to make text stand out. Text can be emphasised using **bold**, *italics* or <u>underlining</u>.
English date format	Day followed by month followed by year. Examples: 30/11/62 30/11/1962 30 Nov 62 30 November 1962.
Enter key (Return key)	A key that moves the cursor down to the next line.

File	A collection of saved data. Examples are text files, word processed files, image files (pictures).
Find and Replace	A technique where the computer searches for a particular word in a document and replaces instances of one word with an alternative word.
File extension	A dot and 3 or 4 characters after a filename, which show the file type. (.doc is the file extension for a Word file.)
Floppy disk	A small portable storage device. It holds very little data and is commonly used for saving small files.
Folder	A storage area in which files can be saved. Creating folders with suitable names allows computer files to be organised logically.
Font size	The size of characters in the document.
Font type	A font is a style/design for the text. Examples are Arial, Times New Roman, Comic Sans.
Format	Changing the layout and appearance of text.
Grammar checker	A tool that checks the grammar within a document and usually tries to provide guidance as to correct usage.
Hardware	The physical parts of a computer workstation that you can see e.g. monitor, keyboard, mouse, printer and the CPU box.
Hover	To position the mouse over an object/area on the screen.
Icon	A small picture representing an object such as a file, folder or program. Toolbar buttons are also referred to as icons, when clicked these make the computer perform a task quickly.
Indent	Text set in from the left or right margin.
Initial capital	A capital letter at the beginning of a word.
Insert	To insert new data in a selected position.
Justify (fully justify)	To align text along the margin on the left and right of the page.
Keyboard	A hardware device used to enter data into a computer.
Line spacing	The amount of vertical space between lines of text.
Load up	See **boot up**.
Lower case	All the characters are in small letters, there are no capital letters.
Margins	The amount of white space from the edge of the paper to the text on the page. In Word the top, bottom, left and right margins can be modified.
Memory	The part of a computer that stores data and programs.

Menu	A list of items.
Monitor	A hardware device that allows the user to view actions being performed. Looks similar to a television screen.
Mouse	A hardware device that allows the user to point and click at things on the monitor.
Mouse pointer	The symbol or pointer visible on the monitor.
My Computer	A folder created in all versions of Windows. File management tasks can be performed through My Computer.
Network	A network links computers together so that they can exchange or share information. A user can send information from one computer to another on the same network.
Operating system	A program that controls the overall activity of a computer.
Page orientation	The way paper is displayed; portrait orientation has the shortest side at the top and landscape orientation has the longest side at the top.
Paragraph marker	A symbol that is displayed when the Show/hide tool is switched on, it shows when the Enter key has been used.
Password	Usually secret, it is a means of allowing a user to log on to a computer system or to open a protected file. Appears as dots on the screen when entered for security reasons.
Ports	The connection points for cables that allow computer hardware to be connected together.
Print Preview	Displays on-screen how a document will look when printed.
Printer	A hardware device that enables data to be printed on to paper. Printed data is referred to as output or hard copy.
Recycle Bin	A storage area created by Windows where deleted files are temporarily held.
Shift key	When pressed together with a letter on the keyboard allows you to key one capital letter.
Shortcut	An icon, usually found on the Desktop screen, which quickly opens an application, file or folder stored elsewhere.
Show/hide	A tool in Word that allows character and paragraph spacing to be displayed on-screen to help check layout.
Shut down	To turn off the computer's operating system.
Spacebar	A key that allows a user to insert a space.
Spell check	A tool in Word that automatically checks that every word is spelt correctly.

Start button	A button on the bottom left of the Taskbar that allows a user to access all the programs on the computer.
Subfolder	A folder inside another folder.
Tab	A set position to which text can be indented using the Tab key on the keyboard.
Tab (in a window)	A window may have a number of tabs, these are the different sections of the window. To view the options in that section, click on the tab name.
Task Pane	A section, usually located on the right-hand side of the screen. It displays a list of recently used files and options available in Word.
Taskbar	A bar usually at the bottom of the screen, running the length of the Desktop screen, it shows which tasks the computer is performing.
Template	A pre-formatted page layout which can contain headers, footers and embedded objects.
Tool tip	When the mouse hovers over an item the program displays a tip, usually on a yellow background, showing the name of an object on the screen.
Upper case	Every letter is a capital letter.
User area	The workspace on a computer for a user to save files. Examples of user areas are: My Documents folder, a network drive, a floppy disk or the C drive.
Username	An identification e.g. name, student number, given to a computer user to identify him or her.
Word processor	A computer program for the creation and manipulation of documents.
Word wrap	Automatic wrapping of a sentence on to the next line without the need to press Enter. This breaks lines automatically between words, so that when the text being entered on the line reaches beyond the right-hand margin, the whole of the last word is transferred to the beginning of the next line.
WYSIWYG	What You See Is What You Get. The data you see on screen appears the same as it will when printed.

Preparation for the assessment

General assessment guidelines for all units

Before the assessment

Before you start a live assessment, complete at least two 'mock exams' in assessment conditions, without help from your tutor or colleagues.

The assessment

- Level 1 assessments are usually divided into four tasks.
- You are allowed a notional duration of 2½ hours for each assessment.
- Before you begin, read through the paper to see what you will need to do.
- You may want to allow yourself about 30 minutes for each task and then 30 minutes to check all your final printouts and saved files.
- Your tutor may allow you to complete an assessment over several consecutive sessions (lessons).
- Once you start an assessment, your tutor cannot give you further teaching, and is not allowed to help you, so make sure you are ready for the assessment before starting a live assessment.
- Your tutor will provide you with a photocopy of the original assignment.
- Printing can be done after the assessment. However, you are advised to print your work whenever there is an instruction to print. When you have printed your work, do not move straight on to the next instruction or task. Check your printout against the instructions in the assignment to make sure that you have carried out each instruction correctly and that the printout matches what you have on the screen.

Headers and footers

- Unless there is a specific instruction, you may use any font size, font type and alignment for headers and footers.

> **TIP!**
>
> Use the **Tab** key or the **spacebar** to insert a few spaces between header and footer items

Your name:
In many assignments you will be asked to enter your name. It is good practice to enter your first and last name.

Filenames:
You are advised to enter filenames using the same case as in the assignment. However, you will not be penalised if you use different case for filenames. Do not enter a full stop after a file or folder name.

Computer-based assessment:
If your work is going to be marked using computer-based assessment, then it is extremely important that you save all files in the correct folder and with the exact filename specified.

During the assessment

- During the assessment you are allowed to use:
  - the Heinemann textbook that you worked through for your learning
  - the Quick reference guides from the Heinemann textbook
  - your own notes
  - handouts from your tutor that cover general IT skills
  - any books that cover general IT skills.
- You are not allowed to use any books, notes, handouts, etc. that are referenced to the assessment objectives of the syllabus.
- You cannot ask your tutor or anyone else for help.
- If there is a technical problem, e.g. something wrong with the computer or printer, then you should inform your tutor/the invigilator.
- Read through the whole task before you start.
- All the instructions are numbered, and many have sub-steps (a, b, c, etc.). Read through the whole step before you start doing anything.
- Follow each instruction in the correct sequence. Do not leave out an instruction intending to do it later.
- Tick each instruction when you have completed it.
- Check that you have completed a step fully and correctly before moving on to the next step.
- Don't rush!
- Enter all data in the same case (i.e. capital/small letters) as in the assignment.
- Enter all data as it is presented in the assignment. Ignore any alternative spelling or grammar suggestions made by the software.
- Any data that you have to type in is presented in bold to help you see what you have to key in. You should not use bold emphasis unless you are told to do so in the assessment.
- Make sure the spell checker is switched on before you start and do a spell check again when you finish.
- If you find an error, you can correct it, but if you leave the checking to your tutor, he or she cannot give you your work back to correct any errors that he or she has found.
- If you notice an error, you can make changes to your work and print again.
- You may print as many draft copies as you wish, but you must remember to destroy any rough or incorrect copies.
- Where there is an instruction to enter your name, or to add your name to a file or folder name, then you must use your own first and last name, not the words 'your name'.
- You will be asked to enter your centre number. You may enter this in any format, e.g. Centre Number 11111, Centre No. 11111, Centre 11111, 11111.

TIP!

Saving: Read through all the instructions for the task before you start work. If you are required to save the file with a different filename, then do so before you start the task. This way you will not save over a file for the previous task.

At the end of the assessment

- Check your printout against the assessment paper. Use a different colour pen/pencil to tick each instruction on the copy of the assessment again.
- Make sure that you have saved all your files.
- Make sure that you have saved with the correct filename.
- Make sure that all your files are saved in the correct user area.
- Make sure every printout has your first and last name on it.
- Arrange your prints – put the final correct version of each printout in the order that they are listed in the assessment.
- Destroy any printouts that you do not wish to be marked (or hand these to your tutor making sure that your tutor knows these are not to be marked!).
- Hand to your tutor:
  - your final printouts in the correct order, you may wish to staple these to keep them secure
  - the copy of the assessment paper
  - the disk where you have saved your files (if you save on disk); if not, tell the tutor where your files are saved on the computer.

Assessment guidelines for Unit 1

- Your tutor will provide you with all the files you need for the assessment.
- Before an assessment, you should create a new folder just for the assessment.

TIP!

Before you start, COPY the folder containing the files into another user area in case you need to open an original file again.

- There will be one folder containing one or more files, and there may be a subfolder containing one or more files.

File management task

- This task may be the first or last task.
- During the assessment, you will need to:
  - rename a folder or a file (change the existing name)
  - create a new folder and give it a name.
  - copy a file from one folder to another
  - move a file from one folder to another
  - delete a file or a folder.
- You are advised to enter file and folder names using the same case as in the assignment. However, you will not be penalised for different use of case for file or folder names.
- Your name: If you are asked to rename a folder using your name, then you should **type your own first and last name**, not the words 'your name'.

- When you have completed the file management task you will need to take a screen print to show that you have carried out all the instructions correctly.
- You may save both screen prints in one document or in separate documents.

TIP!
You must save the screen print(s). The file(s) containing the screen prints do not have to be saved in the folder/subfolder that you will be carrying out the file management tasks in.

- Check the screen printout(s) to make sure that all files and folders and the file and folder names can be clearly seen on the printout.
- If the file or folders and/or the file and folder names are not clear, or the print quality is poor, print again.

e-document production tasks

e-document production is actually word processing.

There will usually be three tasks covering word-processing skills.
- You will create a new document and enter text (approximately 100–130 words).
- You will use a word-processed file provided by OCR, and will be asked to make some changes to this file then save it with a different filename.
- In the new document or in the provided file, you will be required to:
  - create a small table
  - carry out some formatting
  - apply bullets or numbering
  - carry out a word count.

Create a new document.
- Make sure you open a new document. Do not open an existing document that may already have headers and footers or any text.
- Follow each instruction about setting the orientation, font type, font size, margins, line spacing in the correct sequence. Do not leave an instruction intending to do it later.
- Your line endings will probably be different to those on the assessment paper, this is expected. Do **NOT** press Enter at the end of lines within paragraphs!
- Do not enter the text in bold. The text is presented in bold simply to help you to see what to type.
- When asked to insert an automatic date and an automatic filename, do **NOT** type the date or the filename. You **MUST** use the automatic date and automatic filename option in Word.

Edit a provided document.
- Remember the saving tip! Save this file with the new filename before you start working through the task.
- You may be asked to apply a bullet character or numbers to a few lines of text that are already in the document:
  - You may use any style of bullet character or numbering for this.

- In Microsoft Word, when you apply bullets or numbers the text may automatically indent – this is acceptable.
- When you replace a word, remember to use **Replace All** (not **Replace**).

Word count

Carry out the word count **twice** just to be sure that you have done this accurately. Use **CTRL + A** the first time to select all the text, and highlight with the mouse the second time. When you have completed the word count, make a note of the number of words so that you can type the number of words at the end of the document.

Creating a table

When you insert a table in Word, the table borders may extend into the margin space a little – this is acceptable. Reducing the column width is optional.

Good luck

Index